INTRODUCTION

Distinctive Home Designs

Smaller Home Plans is a collection of best-selling smaller homes, including vacation homes, from some of the nation's leading designers and architects. Only quality plans with sound design, functional layout, energy efficiency and affordability have been selected.

This plan book covers a wide range of architectural styles in a popular range of sizes. A broad assortment is presented to match a wide variety of lifestyles and budgets. Each design page features floor plans, a front view of the house and a list of features. All floor plans show room dimensions, exterior dimensions and the interior square footage of the home.

Technical Specifications

At the time these construction drawings were prepared, every effort was made to ensure that these plans and specifications meet nationally recognized building codes (BOCA, Southern Building Code Congress and others). Because national building codes change or vary from area to area some drawing modifications and/or the assistance of a professional designer or architect may be necessary to comply with your local codes or to accommodate specific building site conditions. We advise you to consult with your local building official for information regarding codes governing your area.

Detailed Material Lists

An accurate and detailed material list can save you a considerable amount of time and money. Our material list

gives you the quantity, dimensions and descriptions of the major building materials necessary to construct your home. You'll get faster and more accurate bids from contractors and material suppliers, and you'll save money by paying for only the materials you need. Our package includes the material list, residential building resources, architect's scale, handy calculator, and convenient pen and paper all wrapped neatly in a durable leather portfolio. A material list is available for every plan in this book for $125. Please see page 80 for ordering information.

Blueprint Ordering - Fast and Easy

Your ordering is made simple by following the instructions on page 80. See page 77 for more information on what type of blueprint packages are available and how many plan sets to order.

Your Home, Your Way

The blueprints you receive are a master plan for building your new home. They start you on your way to what may well be the most rewarding experience of your life.

CONTENTS

House on front cover is Plan Number 528-022D-0018 featured on page 52.

Lowe's Home Plans Smaller Homes Edition is published by HDA, Inc. (Home Design ... 63042. All rights reserved. R ... en permission of the publisher ... tist drawings and photos show ... e actual working drawings. Sor ... to the floor plan for accurate ...

D1445683

Quick & Easy Customizing
Make Changes To Your Home Plan In **4** Steps

Here's an affordable and efficient way to make changes to your plan.

1. Select the house plan that most closely meets your needs. Purchase of a reproducible master is necessary in order to make changes to a plan.

2. Call 1-800-373-2646 or e-mail customize@hdainc.com to place your order. Tell the sales representative you're interested in customizing a plan. A $50 nonrefundable consultation fee will be charged. You will then be instructed to complete a customization checklist indicating all the changes you wish to make to your plan. You may attach sketches if necessary. If you proceed with the custom changes the $50 will be credited to the total amount charged.

3. FAX the completed customization checklist to our design consultant. Within 24-48* business hours you will be provided with a written cost estimate to modify your plan. Our design consultant will contact you by phone if you wish to discuss any of your changes in greater detail.

4. Once you approve the estimate, a 75% retainer fee is collected and customization work gets underway. Preliminary drawings can usually be completed within 5-10* business days. Following approval of the preliminary drawings your design changes are completed within 5-10* business days. Your remaining 25% balance due is collected prior to shipment of your completed drawings. You will be shipped five sets of revised blueprints or a reproducible master, plus a customized materials list if required.

BEFORE

AFTER

Sample Modification Pricing Guide
The average prices specified below are provided as examples only. They refer to the most commonly requested changes, and are subject to change without notice. Prices for changes will vary or differ, from the prices below, depending on the number of modifications requested, the plan size, style, quality of original plan, format provided to us (originally drawn by hand or computer), and method of design used by the original designer. To obtain a detailed cost estimate or to get more information, please contact us.

Categories	Average Cost*
Adding or removing living space	Quote required
Adding or removing a garage	Starting at $400
Garage: Front entry to side load or vice versa	Starting at $300
Adding a screened porch	Starting at $280
Adding a bonus room in the attic	Starting at $450
Changing full basement to crawl space or vice versa	Starting at $495
Changing full basement to slab or vice versa	Starting at $495
Changing exterior building material	Starting at $200
Changing roof lines	Starting at $360
Adjusting ceiling height	Starting at $280
Adding, moving or removing an exterior opening	$65 per opening
Adding or removing a fireplace	Starting at $90
Modifying a non-bearing wall or room	$65 per room
Changing exterior walls from 2"x4" to 2"x6"	Starting at $200
Redesigning a bathroom or a kitchen	Starting at $120
Reverse plan right reading	Quote required
Adapting plans for local building code requirements	Quote required
Engineering and Architectural stamping and services	Quote required
Adjust plan for handicapped accessibility	Quote required
Interactive Illustrations (choices of exterior materials)	Quote required
Metric conversion of home plan	Starting at $400

Prices and Terms are subject to change without notice.

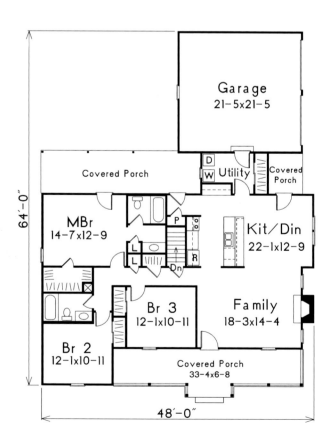

Garage
21-5x21-5

Covered Porch

D
W Utility

Covered Porch

64'-0"

MBr
14-7x12-9

P

L
L

R

Dn

Kit/Din
22-1x12-9

Br 3
12-1x10-11

Family
18-3x14-4

Br 2
12-1x10-11

Covered Porch
33-4x6-8

48'-0"

Plan #528-001D-0031

Country-Style Home With Large Front Porch

Living Area: 1,501 total square feet
Foundation: Basement foundation, drawings also include crawl space and slab foundations
Price Code: B

Special features

- Spacious kitchen with dining area is open to the outdoors
- Convenient utility room is adjacent to garage
- Master bedroom features a private bath, dressing area and access to the large covered porch
- Large family room creates openness
- 3 bedrooms, 2 baths, 2-car side entry garage

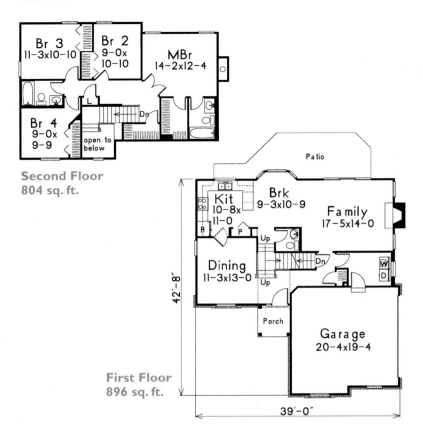

Second Floor
804 sq. ft.

First Floor
896 sq. ft.

Plan #528-007D-0041

Smaller Home
Offers Stylish Exterior

Living Area: 1,700 total square feet
Foundation: Basement foundation
Price Code: B

Special features

- Two-story entry with T-stair is illuminated with a decorative oval window
- Skillfully designed U-shaped kitchen has a built-in pantry
- All bedrooms have generous closet storage and are common to spacious hall with walk-in cedar closet
- 4 bedrooms, 2 1/2 baths, 2-car side entry garage

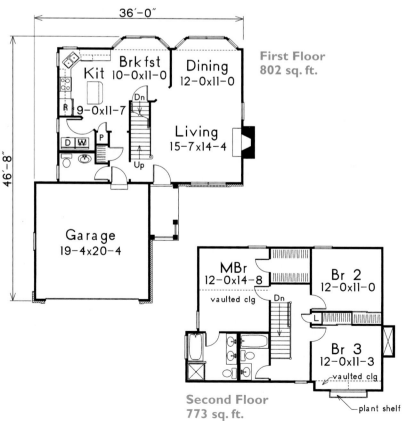

First Floor
802 sq. ft.

36'-0"

46'-8"

Kit
9-0x11-7

Brk fst
10-0x11-0

Dining
12-0x11-0

Living
15-7x14-4

Dn

Up

P

D W

Garage
19-4x20-4

MBr
12-0x14-8
vaulted clg

Br 2
12-0x11-0

Dn

L

Br 3
12-0x11-3
vaulted clg

plant shelf

Second Floor
773 sq. ft.

Plan #528-007D-0054

Stylish Living
For A Narrow Lot

Living Area: 1,575 total square feet
Foundation: Basement foundation, drawings also include crawl space and slab foundations
Price Code: B

Special features

- Inviting porch leads to spacious living and dining rooms
- Kitchen with corner windows features an island snack bar, attractive breakfast room bay, convenient laundry area and built-in pantry
- A luxury bath and walk-in closet adorn the master bedroom suite
- 3 bedrooms, 2 1/2 baths, 2-car garage

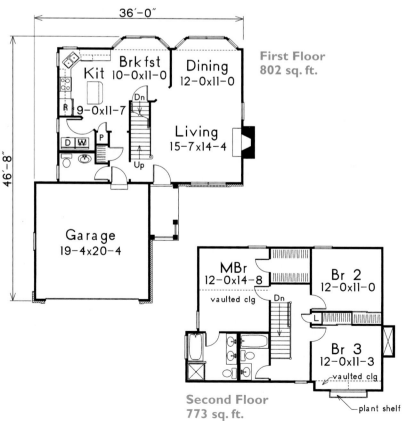

Plan #528-007D-0067

Small Ranch For A Perfect Country Haven

Living Area: 1,761 total square feet
Foundation: Basement foundation
Price Code: B

Special features

- Exterior window dressing, roof dormers and planter boxes provide visual warmth and charm
- Great room boasts a vaulted ceiling, fireplace and opens to a pass-through kitchen
- Master bedroom is vaulted with luxury bath and walk-in closet
- Home features eight separate closets with an abundance of storage
- 4 bedrooms, 2 baths, 2-car side entry garage

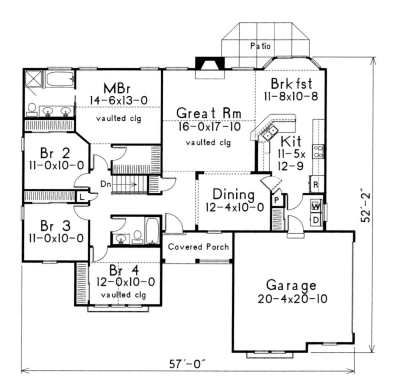

Plan #528-007D-0042

Small Home Is Remarkably Spacious

Living Area: 914 total square feet
Foundation: Basement foundation
Price Code: AA

Special features

- Large porch for leisure evenings
- Dining area with bay window, open stair and pass-through kitchen create openness
- Basement includes generous garage space, storage area, finished laundry and mechanical room
- 2 bedrooms, 1 bath, 2-car drive under garage

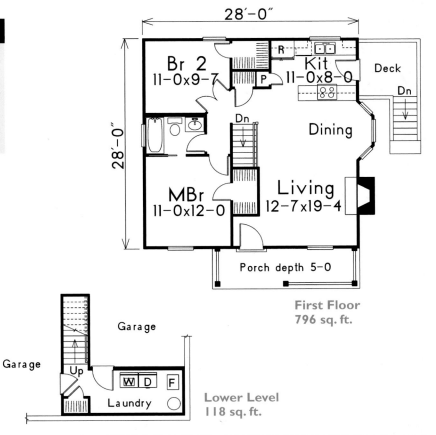

28'-0"

28'-0"

Br 2
11-0x9-7

Kit
11-0x8-0

R

P

Deck

Dn

Dn

Dining

MBr
11-0x12-0

Living
12-7x19-4

Porch depth 5-0

First Floor
796 sq. ft.

Garage

Garage

Up

W D F

Laundry

Lower Level
118 sq. ft.

Plan #528-005D-0001

Classic Ranch Has Grand Appeal With Expansive Porch

Living Area: 1,400 total square feet
Foundation: Basement foundation, drawings also include crawl space foundation
Price Code: B

Special features

- Master bedroom is secluded for privacy
- Large utility room has additional cabinet space
- Covered porch provides an outdoor seating area
- Roof dormers add great curb appeal
- Living room and master bedroom feature vaulted ceilings
- Oversized two-car garage has storage space
- 3 bedrooms, 2 baths, 2-car garage

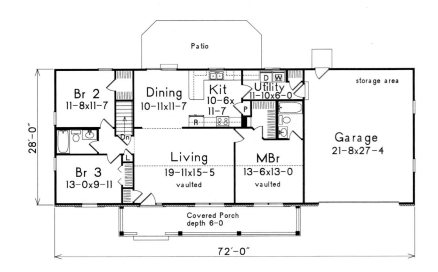

To order blueprints use the form on page 80 or call **1-800-DREAM HOME** (373-2646)

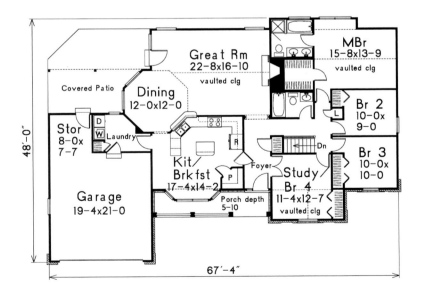

Plan #528-007D-0049

Classic Exterior Employs Innovative Planning

Living Area: 1,791 total square feet
Foundation: Basement foundation, drawings also include crawl space and slab foundations
Price Code: C

Special features

- Vaulted great room and octagon-shaped dining area enjoy a spectacular view of the covered patio
- Kitchen features a pass-through to dining area, center island, large walk-in pantry and breakfast room with large bay window
- Master bedroom is vaulted with sitting area
- 4 bedrooms, 2 baths, 2-car garage with storage

Plan #528-001D-0077

Spacious A-Frame

Living Area: 1,769 total square feet
Foundation: Basement foundation, drawings also include crawl space and slab foundations
Price Code: B

Special features

- Living room boasts an elegant cathedral ceiling and fireplace
- U-shaped kitchen and dining area combine for easy living
- Secondary bedrooms include double closets
- Secluded master bedroom features a sloped ceiling, large walk-in closet and private bath
- 3 bedrooms, 2 baths

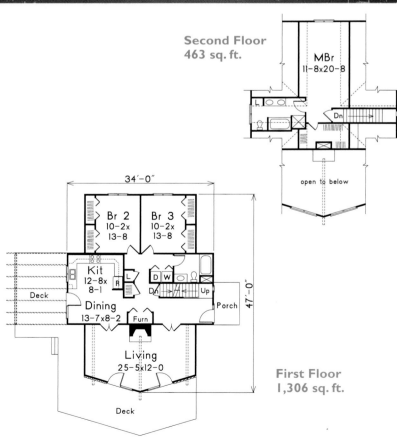

Second Floor
463 sq. ft.

First Floor
1,306 sq. ft.

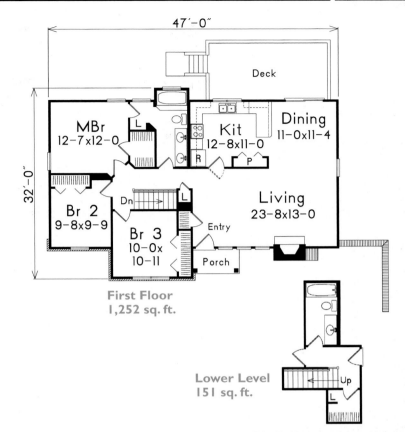

Plan #528-007D-0037

Summer Home
Or Year-Round

Living Area: 1,403 total square feet
Foundation: Basement foundation
Price Code: A

Special features

- Impressive living areas for a modest-sized home
- Special master/hall bath has linen storage, step-up tub and lots of window light
- Spacious closets everywhere you look
- 3 bedrooms, 2 baths, 2-car drive under garage

47'-0"

32'-0"

Deck

MBr
12-7x12-0

Kit
12-8x11-0

Dining
11-0x11-4

L

R

P

Br 2
9-8x9-9

Dn

L

Living
23-8x13-0

Br 3
10-0x
10-11

Entry

Porch

First Floor
1,252 sq. ft.

Lower Level
151 sq. ft.

Up

L

Plan #528-040D-0003

Rambling Country Bungalow

Living Area: 1,475 total square feet
Foundation: Slab foundation, drawings also include crawl space foundation
Price Code: B

Special features

- Family room features a high ceiling and prominent corner fireplace
- Kitchen with island counter and garden window makes a convenient connection between the family and dining rooms
- Hallway leads to three bedrooms all with large walk-in closets
- Covered breezeway joins main house and garage
- Full-width covered porch entry lends a country touch
- 3 bedrooms, 2 baths, 2-car side entry garage

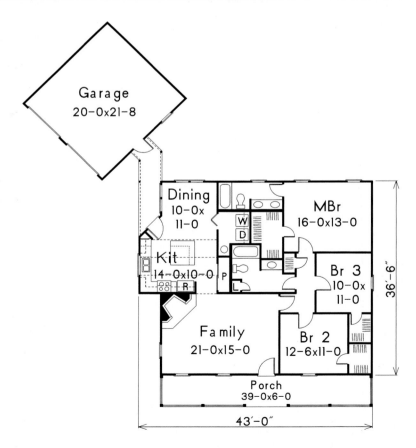

Garage
20-0x21-8

Dining
10-0x
11-0

MBr
16-0x13-0

W
D

Kit
14-0x10-0

Br 3
10-0x
11-0

P

Family
21-0x15-0

Br 2
12-6x11-0

Porch
39-0x6-0

36'-6"

43'-0"

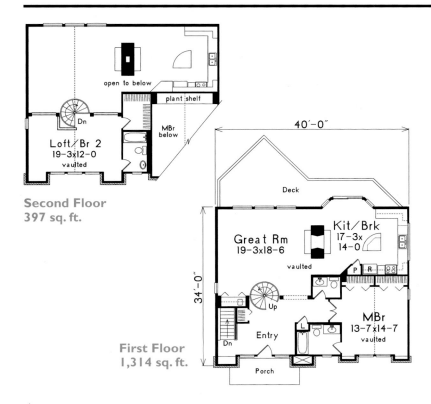

Second Floor
397 sq. ft.

Loft/Br 2
19-3x12-0
vaulted

open to below

plant shelf

MBr
below

Dn

Deck

40'-0"

34'-0"

Great Rm
19-3x18-6
vaulted

Kit/Brk
17-3x
14-0

P R

Up

Dn

Entry

MBr
13-7x14-7
vaulted

Porch

First Floor
1,314 sq. ft.

Plan #528-007D-0028

Ideal Home For Lake, Mountains Or Seaside

Living Area: 1,711 total square feet
Foundation: Basement foundation
Price Code: B

Special features

- Entry leads to a vaulted great room with exposed beams, two-story window wall, fireplace, wet bar and balcony
- Bayed breakfast room shares the fireplace and joins a sun-drenched kitchen and deck
- Vaulted first floor master bedroom features a double-door entry, two closets and bookshelves
- Spiral stairs and a balcony dramatize the loft that doubles as a spacious second bedroom
- 2 bedrooms, 2 1/2 baths

Rear View

Plan #528-007D-0070

Three-Car Apartment Garage With Country Flair

Living Area: 929 total square feet
Foundation: Slab foundation
Price Code: AA

Special features

- Spacious living room with dining area has access to 8' x 12' deck through glass sliding doors
- Splendid U-shaped kitchen features a breakfast bar, oval window above sink and impressive cabinet storage
- Master bedroom enjoys a walk-in closet and large elliptical feature window
- Laundry, storage closet and mechanical space are located off first floor garage
- 2 bedrooms, 1 bath, 3-car side entry garage

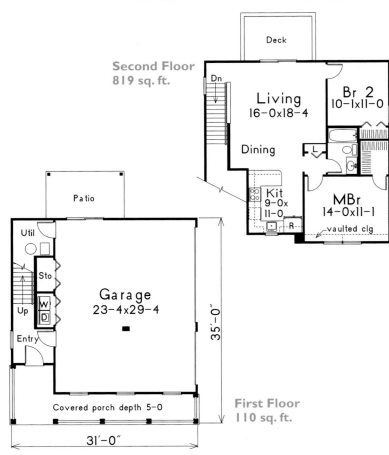

Deck

Second Floor
819 sq. ft.

Dn

Living
16-0x18-4

Br 2
10-1x11-0

Dining

Kit
9-0x
11-0

MBr
14-0x11-1

vaulted clg

Patio

Util

Sto

Up

W D

Entry

Garage
23-4x29-4

35'-0"

Covered porch depth 5-0

31'-0"

First Floor
110 sq. ft.

Plan #528-007D-0060

Distinguished Styling For A Small Lot

Living Area: 1,268 total square feet
Foundation: Basement foundation, drawings also include crawl space and slab foundations
Price Code: B

Special features

- Multiple gables, large porch and arched windows create classy exterior
- Innovative design provides openness in great room, kitchen and breakfast room
- Secondary bedrooms have private hall with bath
- 3 bedrooms, 2 baths, 2-car garage

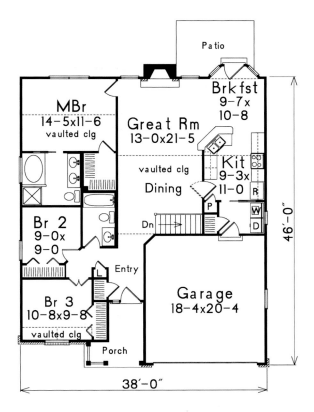

Plan #528-007D-0102

Four Bedroom Living For A Narrow Lot

Living Area: 1,452 total square feet
Foundation: Basement foundation
Price Code: A

Special features

- Large living room features cozy corner fireplace, bayed dining area and access from entry with guest closet
- Forward master bedroom enjoys having its own bath and linen closet
- Three additional bedrooms share a bath with a double-bowl vanity
- 4 bedrooms, 2 baths

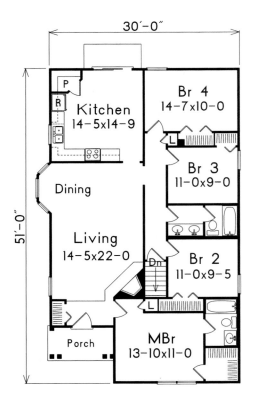

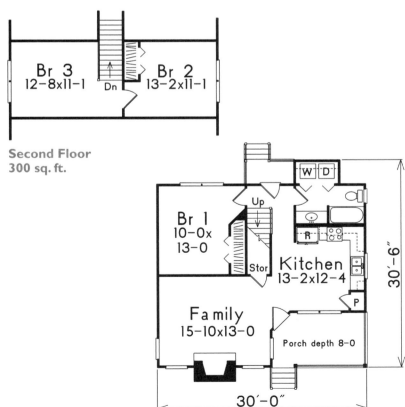

Second Floor
300 sq. ft.

Br 3
12-8x11-1

Dn

Br 2
13-2x11-1

W D

Up

Br 1
10-0x
13-0

Stor

Kitchen
13-2x12-4

R

P

30'-6"

Family
15-10x13-0

Porch depth 8-0

30'-0"

First Floor
728 sq. ft.

Plan #528-040D-0029

Quaint Country Home Is Ideal

Living Area: 1,028 total square feet
Foundation: Crawl space foundation
Price Code: AA

Special features

- Well-designed bath contains laundry facilities
- L-shaped kitchen has a handy pantry
- Tall windows flank family room fireplace
- Cozy covered porch provides unique angled entry into home
- 3 bedrooms, 1 bath

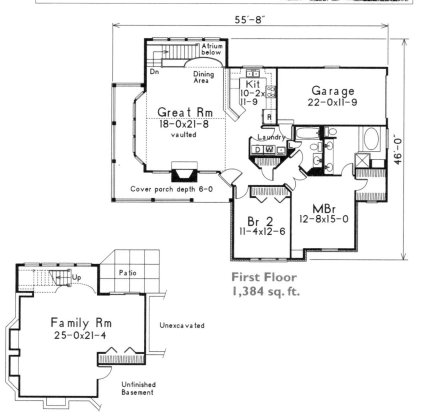

Rear View

Plan #528-007D-0068

Tranquility Of An Atrium Cottage

Living Area: 1,384 total square feet
Foundation: Walk-out basement foundation
Price Code: B

Special features

- Wrap-around country porch for peaceful evenings

- Vaulted great room enjoys a large bay window, stone fireplace, pass-through kitchen and awesome rear views through atrium window wall

- Master bedroom features a double-door entry, walk-in closet and a fabulous bath

- 2 bedrooms, 2 baths, 1-car side entry garage

55'-8"

46'-0"

Atrium below

Dn

Dining Area

Kit
10-2x
11-9

Garage
22-0x11-9

Great Rm
18-0x21-8
vaulted

Laundry

D W

R

Cover porch depth 6-0

Br 2
11-4x12-6

MBr
12-8x15-0

First Floor
1,384 sq. ft.

Up

Patio

Family Rm
25-0x21-4

Unexcavated

Unfinished Basement

**Optional
Lower Level
611 sq. ft.**

Plan #528-017D-0007

Pillared Front Porch Generates Charm And Warmth

Living Area: 1,567 total square feet

Foundation: Partial basement/crawl space foundation, drawings also include slab foundation

Price Code: C

Special features

- Living room flows into the dining room shaped by an angled pass-through into the kitchen
- Cheerful, windowed dining area
- Master bedroom is separated from other bedrooms for privacy
- 3 bedrooms, 2 baths, 2-car side entry garage

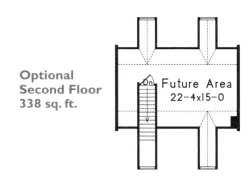

Optional Second Floor 338 sq. ft.

Future Area 22-4x15-0

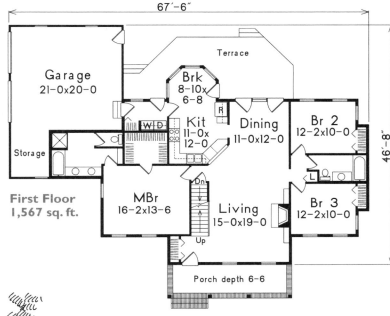

67'-6"

Terrace

Garage 21-0x20-0

Brk 8-10x 6-8

Kit 11-0x 12-0

Dining 11-0x12-0

Br 2 12-2x10-0

Storage

W D

MBr 16-2x13-6

Living 15-0x19-0

Br 3 12-2x10-0

46'-8"

First Floor 1,567 sq. ft.

Porch depth 6-6

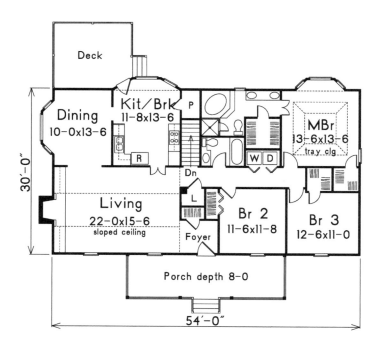

Deck

Dining
10-0x13-6

Kit/Brk
11-8x13-6

P

MBr
13-6x13-6
tray clg

W D

30'-0"

Living
22-0x15-6
sloped ceiling

Dn

L

Foyer

Br 2
11-6x11-8

Br 3
12-6x11-0

Porch depth 8-0

54'-0"

Plan #528-053D-0002

Bay Window Graces X Luxury Master Bedroom

Living Area: 1,668 total square feet
Foundation: Basement foundation
Price Code: C

Special features

- Large bay windows grace the breakfast area, master bedroom and dining room
- Extensive walk-in closets and storage spaces are located throughout the home
- Handy covered entry porch
- Large living room has a fireplace, built-in bookshelves and sloped ceiling
- 3 bedrooms, 2 baths, 2-car drive under garage

Plan #528-001D-0040

Perfect Home For A Small Family

Living Area: 864 total square feet
Foundation: Crawl space foundation, drawings also include basement and slab foundations
Price Code: AAA

Special features

- L-shaped kitchen with convenient pantry is adjacent to dining area
- Easy access to laundry area, linen closet and storage closet
- Both bedrooms include ample closet space
- 2 bedrooms, 1 bath

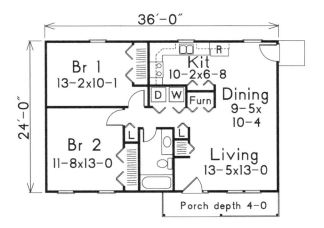

36'-0"

24'-0"

Br 1
13-2x10-1

Kit
10-2x6-8

Dining
9-5x10-4

Br 2
11-8x13-0

Living
13-5x13-0

Porch depth 4-0

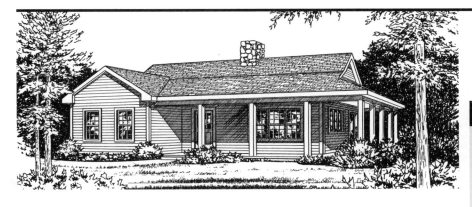

Plan #528-058D-0030

Vaulted Ceiling Adds Spaciousness

Living Area: 990 total square feet
Foundation: Crawl space foundation
Price Code: AA

Special features

- Wrap-around porch on two sides of this home
- Covered porch surrounding one side of this home maintains privacy
- Space for efficiency washer and dryer unit for convenience
- 2 bedrooms, 1 bath

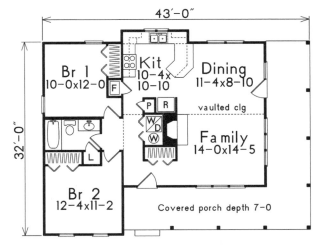

43'-0"

32'-0"

Br 1
10-0x12-0

Kit
10-4x10-10

Dining
11-4x8-10

vaulted clg

Family
14-0x14-5

Br 2
12-4x11-2

Covered porch depth 7-0

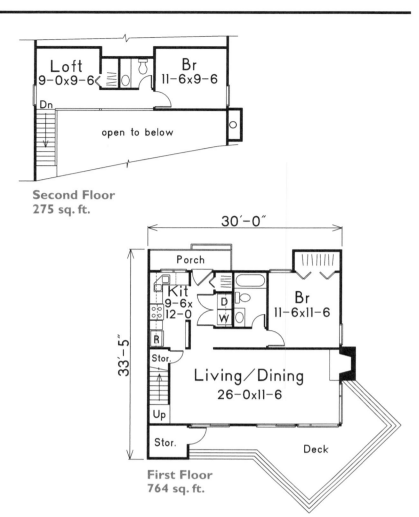

Loft
9-0x9-6

Br
11-6x9-6

Dn

open to below

Second Floor
275 sq. ft.

Plan #528-022D-0001

A Vacation Home For All Seasons

Living Area: 1,039 total square feet
Foundation: Crawl space foundation
Price Code: AA

Special features

- Cathedral construction provides the maximum in living area openness
- Expansive glass viewing walls
- Two decks, front and back
- Charming second story loft arrangement
- Simple, low-maintenance construction
- 2 bedrooms, 1 1/2 baths

30'-0"

33'-5"

Porch

Kit
9-6x
12-0

R

Stor.

Br
11-6x11-6

Living/Dining
26-0x11-6

Up

Stor.

Deck

First Floor
764 sq. ft.

Plan #528-007D-0036

Openness Reflects Relaxed Lifestyle

Living Area: 1,330 total square feet
Foundation: Basement foundation
Price Code: A

Special features

- Vaulted living room is open to bayed dining room and kitchen creating an ideal space for entertaining
- Two bedrooms, a bath and linen closet complete the first floor and are easily accessible
- The second floor offers two bedrooms with walk-in closets, a very large storage room and an opening with louvered doors which overlooks the living room
- 4 bedrooms, 2 baths, 1-car garage

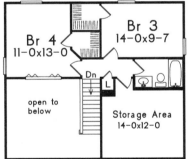

Second Floor
446 sq. ft.

Br 4
11-0x13-0

Br 3
14-0x9-7

Dn   L

open to below

Storage Area
14-0x12-0

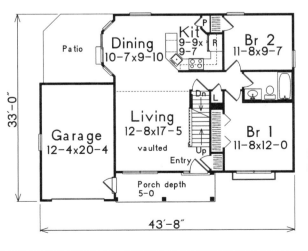

Patio

Dining
10-7x9-10

Kit
9-9x
9-7

P
R

Br 2
11-8x9-7

Dn   L

Garage
12-4x20-4

Living
12-8x17-5
vaulted

Up

Br 1
11-8x12-0

Entry

33'-0"

Porch depth
5-0

43'-8"

First Floor
884 sq. ft.

Plan #528-058D-0006

Year-Round Or Weekend Getaway Home

Living Area: 1,339 total square feet
Foundation: Crawl space foundation
Price Code: A

Special features

- Full-length covered porch enhances front facade
- Vaulted ceiling and stone fireplace add drama to the family room
- Walk-in closets in the bedrooms provide ample storage space
- Combined kitchen/dining area adjoins the family room for the perfect entertaining space
- 3 bedrooms, 2 1/2 baths

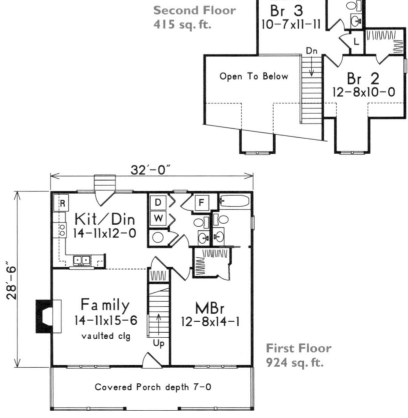

Second Floor
415 sq. ft.

Loft/
Br 3
10-7x11-11

Open To Below

Dn

Br 2
12-8x10-0

32'-0"

R

Kit/Din
14-11x12-0

D W F

28'-6"

Family
14-11x15-6
vaulted clg

Up

MBr
12-8x14-1

First Floor
924 sq. ft.

Covered Porch depth 7-0

Plan #528-007D-0031

Innovative Ranch Has Cozy Corner Patio

Living Area: 1,092 total square feet
Foundation: Basement foundation
Price Code: AA

Special features

- Box window and inviting porch with dormers create a charming facade
- Eat-in kitchen offers a pass-through breakfast bar, corner window wall to patio, pantry and convenient laundry with half bath
- Master bedroom features a double-door entry and walk-in closet
- 3 bedrooms, 1 1/2 baths, 1-car garage

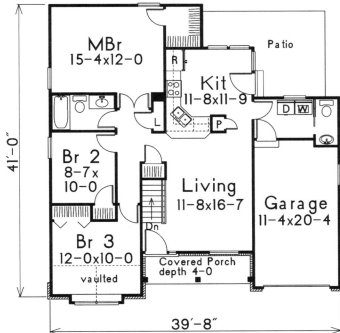

Plan #528-001D-0021

Classic Ranch, Pleasant Covered Front Porch

Living Area: 1,416 total square feet
Foundation: Crawl space foundation, drawings also include basement foundation
Price Code: A

Special features

- Excellent floor plan eases traffic
- Master bedroom features private bath
- Foyer opens to both formal living room and informal great room
- Great room has access to the outdoors through sliding doors
- 3 bedrooms, 2 baths, 2-car garage

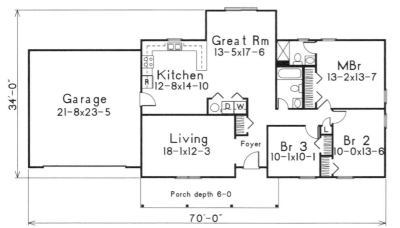

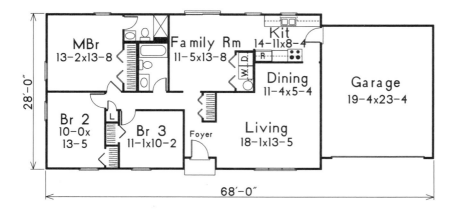

Plan #528-001D-0023

Roomy Ranch For Easy Living

Living Area: 1,343 total square feet
Foundation: Crawl space foundation, drawings also include basement foundation
Price Code: A

Special features

- Separate and convenient family, living and dining areas
- Nice-sized master bedroom enjoys a large closet and private bath
- Foyer with convenient coat closet opens into combined living and dining rooms
- Family room has access to the outdoors through sliding glass doors
- 3 bedrooms, 2 baths, 2-car garage

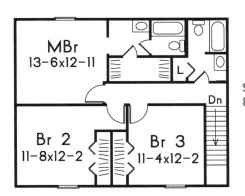

Second Floor
832 sq. ft.

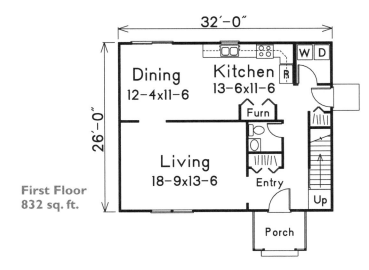

First Floor
832 sq. ft.

Plan #528-001D-0092

Compact Two-Story With All The Conveniences

Living Area: 1,664 total square feet
Foundation: Crawl space foundation, drawings also include basement and slab foundations
Price Code: B

Special features

- Master bedroom includes private bath, dressing area and walk-in closet
- Spacious rooms throughout
- Kitchen features handy side entrance, adjacent laundry room and coat closet
- 3 bedrooms, 2 1/2 baths

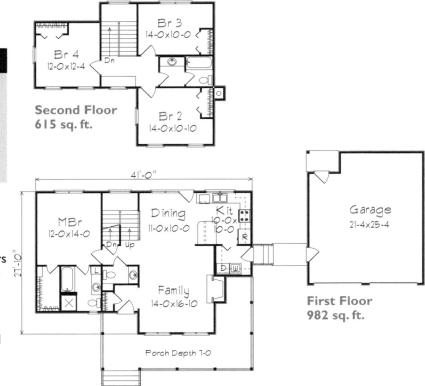

Second Floor
615 sq. ft.

Br 4
12-0x12-4

Br 3
14-0x10-0

Br 2
14-0x10-10

Dn

41'-0"

27'-10"

MBr
12-0x14-0

Dn Up

Dining
11-0x10-0

Kit
10-0x
10-0

R

Family
14-0x16-10

Garage
21-4x25-4

First Floor
982 sq. ft.

Porch Depth 7-0

Plan #528-040D-0027

Country Style With Wrap-Around Porch

Living Area: 1,597 total square feet
Foundation: Basement foundation
Price Code: C

Special features

- Spacious family room includes fireplace and coat closet
- Open kitchen and dining room provide breakfast bar and access to the outdoors
- Convenient laundry area is located near kitchen
- Secluded master bedroom with walk-in closet and private bath
- 4 bedrooms, 2 1/2 baths, 2-car detached garage

Plan #528-053D-0044

Open Living Area Adds Drama To Home

Living Area: 1,340 total square feet
Foundation: Slab foundation, drawings also include crawl space foundation
Price Code: A

Special features

- Master bedroom has a private bath and walk-in closet
- Recessed entry leads to the vaulted family room that shares a see-through fireplace with the kitchen/dining area
- Garage includes a handy storage area
- Convenient laundry closet is in the kitchen
- 3 bedrooms, 2 baths, 2-car side entry garage

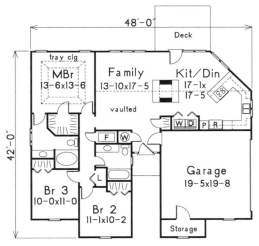

Plan #528-058D-0024

Efficient Kitchen Layout

Living Area: 1,598 total square feet
Foundation: Basement foundation
Price Code: B

Special features

- Additional storage area in garage
- Double-door entry into master bedroom with luxurious master bath
- Entry opens into large family room with vaulted ceiling and open stairway to basement
- 3 bedrooms, 2 baths, 2-car garage

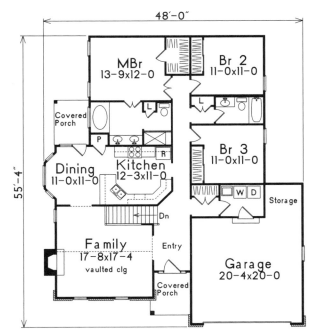

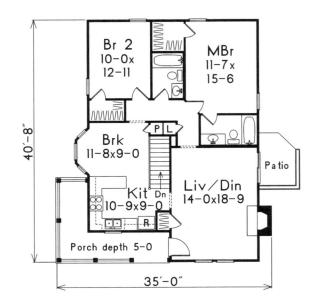

Plan #528-007D-0105

Stylish Retreat For A Narrow Lot

Living Area: 1,084 total square feet
Foundation: Basement foundation
Price Code: AA

Special features

- Delightful country porch for quiet evenings
- The living room offers a front feature window which invites the sun and includes a fireplace and dining area with private patio
- The U-shaped kitchen features lots of cabinets and bayed breakfast room with built-in pantry
- Both bedrooms have walk-in closets and access to their own bath
- 2 bedrooms, 2 baths

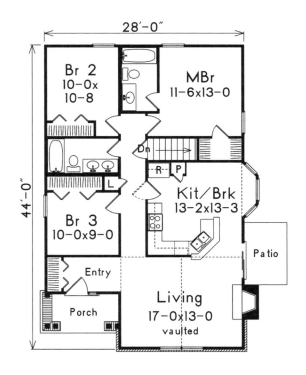

Plan #528-007D-0107

Three Bedroom Luxury In A Small Home

Living Area: 1,161 total square feet
Foundation: Basement foundation
Price Code: AA

Special features

- Brickwork and feature window add elegance to home for a narrow lot
- Living room enjoys a vaulted ceiling, fireplace and opens to kitchen
- U-shaped kitchen offers a breakfast area with bay window, snack bar and built-in pantry
- 3 bedrooms, 2 baths

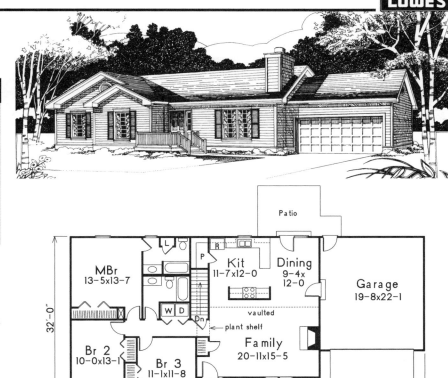

Plan #528-001D-0030

Spacious And Open Family Living Area

Living Area: 1,416 total square feet
Foundation: Basement foundation, drawings also include crawl space and slab foundations
Price Code: A

Special features

- Family room includes fireplace, elevated plant shelf and vaulted ceiling
- Patio is accessible from dining area and garage
- Centrally located laundry area
- Oversized walk-in pantry
- 3 bedrooms, 2 baths, 2-car garage

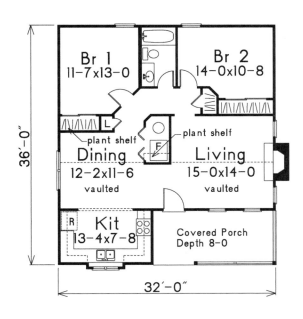

Plan #528-058D-0003

Quaint Cottage With Inviting Front Porch

Living Area: 1,020 total square feet
Foundation: Slab foundation
Price Code: AA

Special features

- Living room is warmed by a fireplace
- Dining and living rooms are enhanced by vaulted ceilings and plant shelves
- U-shaped kitchen with large window over the sink
- 2 bedrooms, 1 bath

Plan #528-017D-0008

Rustic Stone Exterior

Living Area: 1,466 total square feet
Foundation: Basement foundation, drawings also include slab foundation
Price Code: B

Special features

- Energy efficient home with 2" x 6" exterior walls
- Foyer separates the living room from the dining room and contains a generous coat closet
- Large living room features a corner fireplace, bay window and pass-through to the kitchen
- Informal breakfast area opens to a large terrace through sliding glass doors which brighten area
- Master bedroom has a large walk-in closet and private bath
- 3 bedrooms, 2 baths, 2-car garage

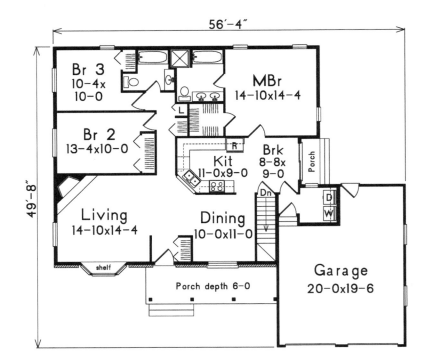

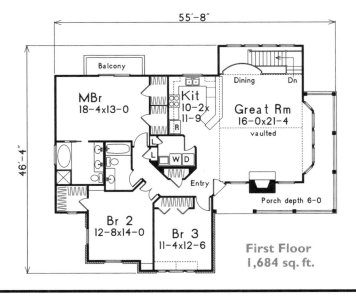

Rear View

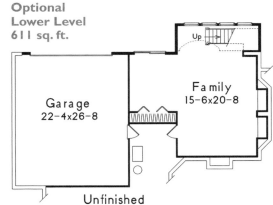

Optional Lower Level 611 sq. ft.

Garage
22-4x26-8

Family
15-6x20-8

Up

Unfinished

Plan #528-007D-0075

A Special Home For Views

Living Area: 1,684 total square feet

Foundation: Walk-out basement foundation

Price Code: B

Special features

- Delightful wrap-around porch is anchored by a full masonry fireplace
- The vaulted great room includes a large bay window, fireplace, dining balcony and atrium window wall
- Double walk-in closets, large luxury bath and sliding doors to exterior balcony are a few fantastic features of the master bedroom
- 3 bedrooms, 2 baths, 2-car drive under garage

55'-8"

46'-4"

Balcony

MBr
18-4x13-0

Kit
10-2x
11-9

Dining

Dn

Great Rm
16-0x21-4
vaulted

L

W D

Entry

Porch depth 6-0

Br 2
12-8x14-0

Br 3
11-4x12-6

**First Floor
1,684 sq. ft.**

LOWE'S

Plan #528-058D-0013

Comfortable Vacation Retreat

Living Area: 1,073 total square feet
Foundation: Crawl space foundation
Price Code: AA

Special features

- Home includes a lovely covered front porch and a screened porch off dining area
- Attractive box window brightens the kitchen
- Space for efficiency washer and dryer is located conveniently between the bedrooms
- Family room is spotlighted by a fireplace with flanking bookshelves and spacious vaulted ceiling
- 2 bedrooms, 1 bath

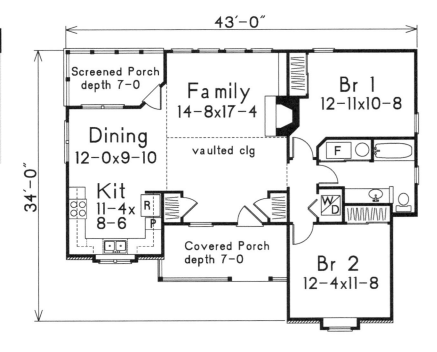

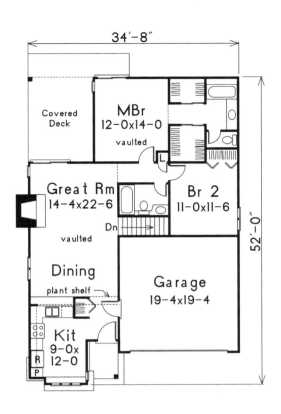

34'-8"

52'-0"

Covered Deck

MBr
12-0x14-0
vaulted

Great Rm
14-4x22-6
vaulted

Dn

Dining
plant shelf

Br 2
11-0x11-6

Garage
19-4x19-4

Kit
9-0x
12-0

Plan #528-022D-0024

Charming Exterior & Cozy Interior

Living Area: 1,127 total square feet
Foundation: Basement foundation
Price Code: AA

Special features

- Plant shelf joins kitchen and dining room
- Vaulted master bedroom has double walk-in closets, deck access and private bath
- Great room features vaulted ceiling, fireplace and sliding doors to covered deck
- Ideal home for a narrow lot
- 2 bedrooms, 2 baths, 2-car garage

Plan #528-001D-0072

Peaceful Shaded Front Porch

Living Area: 1,288 total square feet
Foundation: Crawl space foundation, drawings also include basement and slab foundations
Price Code: A

Special features

- Kitchen, dining area and great room join to create an open living space
- Master bedroom includes private bath
- Secondary bedrooms include ample closet space
- Hall bath features convenient laundry closet
- Dining room accesses the outdoors
- 3 bedrooms, 2 baths

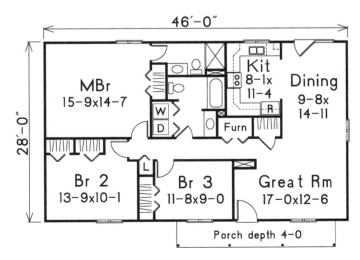

46'-0"

28'-0"

MBr
15-9x14-7

W
D

Kit
8-1x
11-4

Furn

Dining
9-8x
14-11

Br 2
13-9x10-1

Br 3
11-8x9-0

Great Rm
17-0x12-6

Porch depth 4-0

Plan #528-045D-0017

Dormer And Covered Porch Add To Country Charm

Living Area: 954 total square feet
Foundation: Basement foundation
Price Code: AA

Special features

- Kitchen has cozy bayed eating area
- Master bedroom has a walk-in closet and private bath
- Large great room has access to the back porch
- Convenient coat closet near front entry
- 3 bedrooms, 2 baths

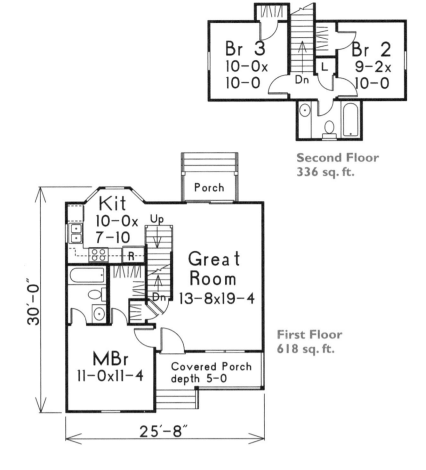

Second Floor
336 sq. ft.

First Floor
618 sq. ft.

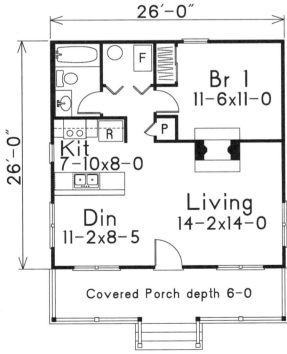

26'-0"

26'-0"

Br 1
11-6x11-0

F

Kit
7-10x8-0

R

P

Din
11-2x8-5

Living
14-2x14-0

Covered Porch depth 6-0

Plan #528-058D-0010

Small And Cozy Cabin

Living Area: 676 total square feet
Foundation: Crawl space foundation
Price Code: AAA

Special features

- See-through fireplace between bedroom and living area adds character
- Combined dining and living areas create an open feeling
- Full-length front covered porch is perfect for enjoying the outdoors
- Additional storage available in utility room
- 1 bedroom, 1 bath

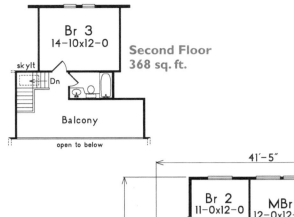

Second Floor
368 sq. ft.

Br 3
14-10x12-0

skylt

Dn

Balcony

open to below

Plan #528-017D-0010

Dramatic Expanse Of Windows

Living Area: 1,660 total square feet
Foundation: Partial basement/crawl space foundation, drawings also include slab foundation
Price Code: C

Special features

- Convenient gear and equipment room
- Spacious living and dining rooms look even larger with the openness of the foyer and kitchen
- Large wrap-around deck is a great plus for outdoor living
- Broad balcony overlooks living and dining rooms
- 3 bedrooms, 3 baths

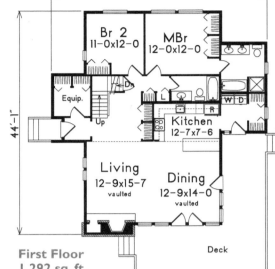

41'-5"

44'-1"

Br 2
11-0x12-0

MBr
12-0x12-0

Equip.

Dn

Up

L

W D

R

Kitchen
12-7x7-6

Living
12-9x15-7
vaulted

Dining
12-9x14-0
vaulted

Deck

First Floor
1,292 sq. ft.

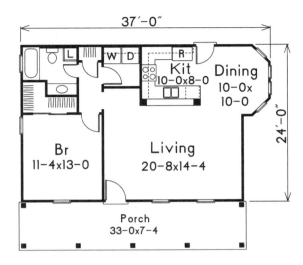

Plan #528-037D-0017

Large Front Porch Adds Welcoming Appeal

Living Area: 829 total square feet
Foundation: Slab foundation
Price Code: AAA

Special features

- U-shaped kitchen opens into living area by a 42" high counter
- Oversized bay window and French door accent dining room
- Gathering space is created by the large living room
- Convenient utility room and linen closet
- 1 bedroom, 1 bath

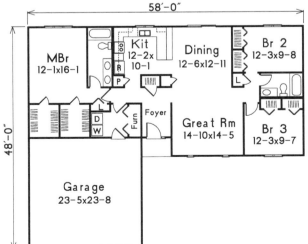

Plan #528-001D-0069

Beauty And Practicality Designed As One

Living Area: 1,504 total square feet
Foundation: Crawl space foundation, drawings also include basement and slab foundations
Price Code: B

Special features

- Private master bedroom features double walk-in closets, linen closet and bath
- Laundry room is conveniently located near garage
- Open great room and dining area create a spacious living atmosphere
- Generous closet space in secondary bedrooms
- Kitchen features breakfast bar, pantry and storage closet
- 3 bedrooms, 2 baths, 2-car garage

Plan #528-001D-0091

Layout Features All The Essentials For Comfortable Living

Living Area: 1,344 total square feet
Foundation: Crawl space foundation, drawings also include basement and slab foundations
Price Code: A

Special features

- Kitchen has side entry, laundry area, pantry and joins family/dining area
- Master bedroom includes a private bath
- Linen and storage closets in hall
- Covered porch opens to the spacious living room with a handy coat closet
- 3 bedrooms, 2 baths

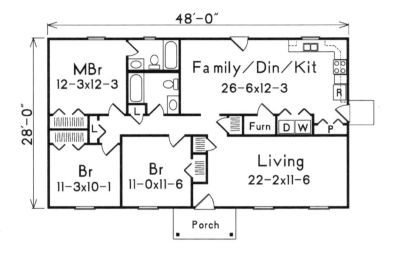

Plan #528-058D-0012

Flexible Layout For Various Uses

Living Area: 1,143 total square feet
Foundation: Crawl space foundation
Price Code: AA

Special features

- Enormous stone fireplace in family room adds warmth and character
- Spacious kitchen with breakfast bar overlooks family room
- Separate dining area is great for entertaining
- Vaulted family room and kitchen create an open atmosphere
- 2 bedrooms, 1 bath

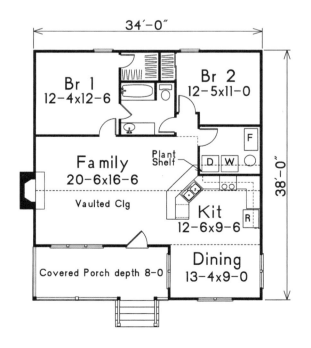

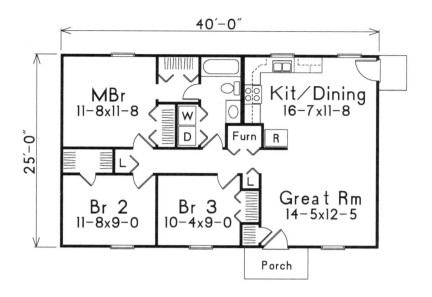

Plan #528-001D-0041

Open Living Area Creates Comfortable Atmosphere

Living Area: 1,000 total square feet
Foundation: Crawl space foundation, drawings also include basement and slab foundations
Price Code: AA

Special features

- Bath includes convenient closeted laundry area
- Master bedroom includes double closets and private access to bath
- Foyer features handy coat closet
- L-shaped kitchen provides easy access outdoors
- 3 bedrooms, 1 bath

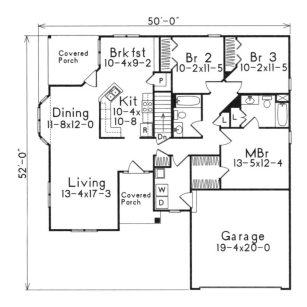

50'-0"

52'-0"

Covered Porch

Brk fst
10-4x9-2

Br 2
10-2x11-5

Br 3
10-2x11-5

Kit
10-4x
10-8

Dining
11-8x12-0

P

R

Dn

L L

Living
13-4x17-3

Covered Porch

W
D

MBr
13-5x12-4

Garage
19-4x20-0

Plan #528-058D-0022

Designed For Handicap Access

Living Area: 1,578 total square feet
Foundation: Basement foundation
Price Code: B

Special features

- Plenty of closet, linen and storage space
- Covered porches in the front and rear of home add charm to this design
- Open floor plan has a unique angled layout
- 3 bedrooms, 2 baths, 2-car garage

Plan #528-058D-0021

Graciously Designed Traditional Ranch

Living Area: 1,477 total square feet
Foundation: Basement foundation
Price Code: A

Special features

- Oversized porch provides protection from the elements
- Innovative kitchen employs step-saving design
- Kitchen has snack bar which opens to the breakfast room with bay window
- 3 bedrooms, 2 baths, 2-car side entry garage with storage area

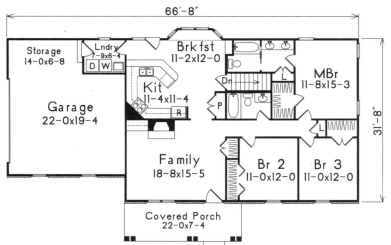

66'-8"

31'-8"

Storage
14-0x6-8

Lndry
7-9x6-4

D W

Brk fst
11-2x12-0

Kit
11-4x11-4

Dn

P

R

MBr
11-8x15-3

L

L

Garage
22-0x19-4

Family
18-8x15-5

Br 2
11-0x12-0

Br 3
11-0x12-0

Covered Porch
22-0x7-4

Plan #528-001D-0018

Front Porch And Center Gable Add Style To This Ranch

Living Area: 988 total square feet
Foundation: Basement foundation, drawings also include crawl space foundation
Price Code: AA

Special features

- Pleasant covered porch entry
- The kitchen, living and dining areas are combined to maximize space
- Entry has convenient coat closet
- Laundry closet is located adjacent to bedrooms
- 3 bedrooms, 1 bath, 1-car garage

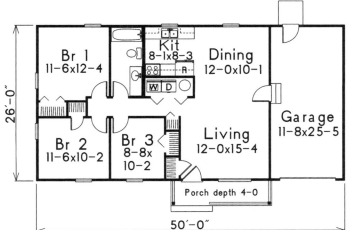

Plan #528-041D-0004

Vaulted Ceiling Frames Circle-Top Window

Living Area: 1,195 total square feet
Foundation: Basement foundation
Price Code: AA

Special features

- Dining room opens onto the patio
- Master bedroom features a vaulted ceiling, private bath and walk-in closet
- Coat closets are located by both the entrances
- Convenient secondary entrance is located at the back of the garage
- 3 bedrooms, 2 baths, 2-car garage

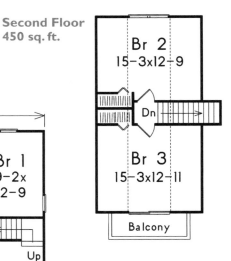

Second Floor
450 sq. ft.

Br 2
15-3x12-9

Dn

Br 3
15-3x12-11

Balcony

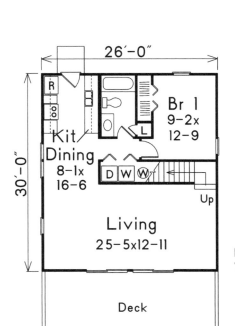

26'-0"

R

Br 1
9-2x
12-9

Kit
Dining
8-1x
16-6

D W W

Up

30'-0"

Living
25-5x12-11

First Floor
780 sq. ft.

Deck

Plan #528-001D-0087

Perfect Vacation Home

Living Area: 1,230 total square feet
Foundation: Crawl space foundation, drawings also include slab foundation
Price Code: A

Special features

- Spacious living room accesses huge deck
- Bedroom #3 features a balcony over-looking the deck
- Kitchen with dining area accesses the outdoors
- Washer and dryer are tucked under the stairs
- 3 bedrooms, 1 bath

Br 2
10–0x11–0
vaulted clg

Br 3
10–0x11–0
vaulted clg

Gathering Rm
15–5x15–5
vaulted clg

Dn

Second Floor
672 sq. ft.

51'–0"

Covered Porch
depth 9-0

vaulted clg

Stor

D
W

Dining
10–3x10–5

Kit
10x10

MBr
12–0x17–6
vaulted clg

Up
P

R

Garage
13–5x22–0

Dn

Living
20–9x15–6

50'–7"

Covered Porch
depth 8-0

First Floor
1,112 sq. ft.

Plan #528-068D-0003

Outdoor Living Area Created By Wrap-Around Covered Porch

Living Area: 1,784 total square feet
Foundation: Basement foundation, drawings also include crawl space foundation
Price Code: B

Special features

- Spacious living area with corner fireplace offers a cheerful atmosphere with large windows
- Large second floor gathering room is great for children's play area
- Secluded master bedroom has separate porch entrances and a large master bath with walk-in closet
- 3 bedrooms, 2 1/2 baths, 1-car garage

Plan #528-007D-0038

Dining With A View

Living Area: 1,524 total square feet

Foundation: Basement foundation, drawings also include crawl space and slab foundations

Price Code: B

Special features

- Delightful balcony overlooks two-story entry illuminated by oval window
- Roomy first floor master bedroom offers quiet privacy
- All bedrooms feature one or more walk-in closets
- 3 bedrooms, 2 1/2 baths, 2-car garage

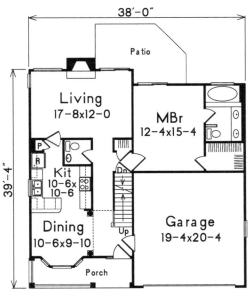

38'-0"

Patio

Living
17-8x12-0

MBr
12-4x15-4

39'-4"

Kit
10-6x
10-6

Dn

Dining
10-6x9-10

Up

Garage
19-4x20-4

Porch

First Floor
951 sq. ft.

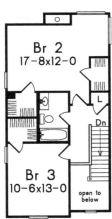

Br 2
17-8x12-0

Dn

L

Br 3
10-6x13-0

open to below

Second Floor
573 sq. ft.

Plan #528-058D-0016

Lovely, Spacious Floor Plan

Living Area: 1,558 total square feet
Foundation: Basement foundation
Price Code: B

Special features

- The spacious utility room is located conveniently between the garage and kitchen/dining area
- Bedrooms are separated from the living area by hallway
- Enormous living area with fireplace and vaulted ceiling opens to the kitchen and dining area
- Master bedroom is enhanced with large bay window, walk-in closet and private bath
- 3 bedrooms, 2 baths, 2-car garage

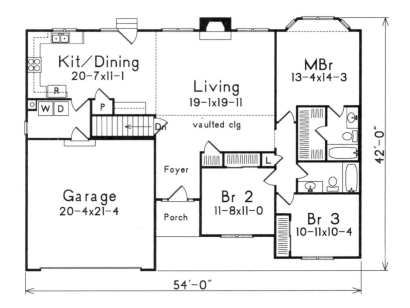

SPARR

Plan #528-001D-0086

Open Living Area

Living Area: 1,154 total square feet
Foundation: Crawl space foundation, drawings also include slab foundation
Price Code: AA

Special features

- U-shaped kitchen features a large break-fast bar and handy laundry area
- Private second floor bedrooms share half bath
- Large living/dining area opens to deck
- 3 bedrooms, 1 1/2 baths

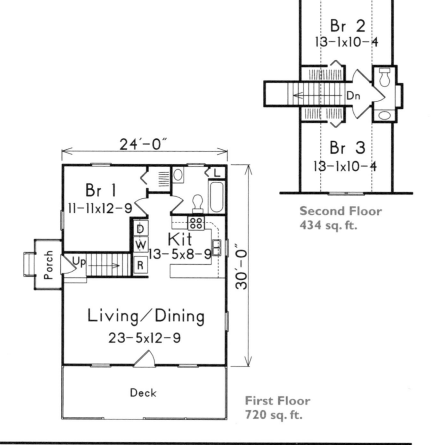

Br 2
13-1x10-4

Dn

Br 3
13-1x10-4

Second Floor
434 sq. ft.

24'-0"

Br 1
11-11x12-9

Porch

Up

D

W

R

Kit
13-5x8-9

30'-0"

Living/Dining
23-5x12-9

Deck

First Floor
720 sq. ft.

Plan #528-010D-0007

Large Windows Grace This Split-Level Home

Living Area: 1,427 total square feet
Foundation: Basement foundation
Price Code: A

Special features

- Practical storage space is situated in the garage
- Convenient laundry closet is located on the lower level
- Kitchen and dining area both have sliding doors that access the deck
- Large expansive space is created by vaulted living and dining rooms
- 3 bedrooms, 2 baths, 2-car drive under garage

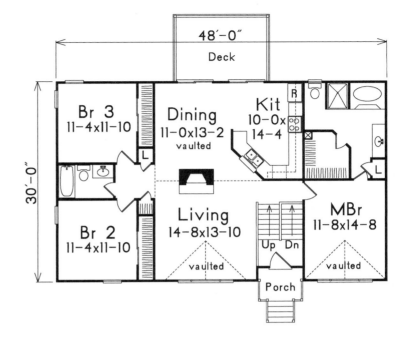

J.N. HANSEN S.D.G.

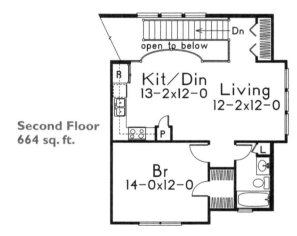

Second Floor
664 sq. ft.

Dn

open to below

R

Kit/Din
13-2x12-0

Living
12-2x12-0

P

Br
14-0x12-0

L

Plan #528-007D-0073

Apartment Garage
With Atrium

Living Area: 902 total square feet
Foundation: Slab foundation
Price Code: AA

Special features

- Vaulted entry with laundry room leads to a spacious second floor apartment
- The large living room features an entry coat closet, L-shaped kitchen with pantry and dining area/balcony overlooking atrium window wall
- Roomy bedroom with walk-in closet is convenient to hall bath
- 1 bedroom, 1 bath, 2-car side entry garage

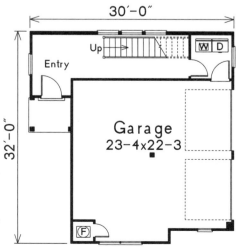

30'-0"

Up

W D

Entry

32'-0"

Garage
23-4x22-3

F

First Floor
238 sq. ft.

Plan #528-022D-0019

Large Corner Deck Lends Way To Outdoor Living Area

Living Area: 1,283 total square feet
Foundation: Basement foundation
Price Code: A

Special features

- Vaulted breakfast room has sliding doors that open onto deck
- Kitchen features convenient corner sink and pass-through to dining room
- Open living atmosphere in dining area and great room
- Vaulted great room features a fireplace
- 3 bedrooms, 2 baths, 2-car garage

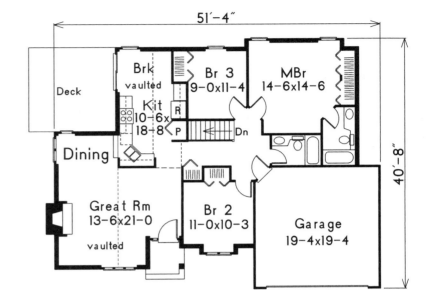

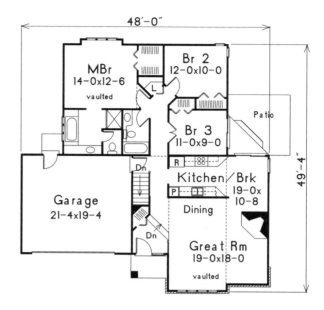

Plan #528-022D-0018

Great Room Window Adds Character Inside And Out ✕

Living Area: 1,368 total square feet
Foundation: Basement foundation
Price Code: A

Special features

- Entry foyer steps down to open living area which combines great room and formal dining area
- Vaulted master bedroom includes a box-bay window, large vanity, separate tub and shower
- Cozy breakfast area features direct access to the patio and pass-through kitchen
- Handy linen closet is located in the hall
- 3 bedrooms, 2 baths, 2-car garage

Floor plan labels:
48'-0"
49'-4"
MBr 14-0x12-6 vaulted
Br 2 12-0x10-0
Br 3 11-0x9-0
Patio
Garage 21-4x19-4
Kitchen/Brk 19-0x10-8
Dining
Great Rm 19-0x18-0 vaulted
Dn

Plan #528-001D-0090

Secluded Bedroom Makes Great Guest Quarters

Living Area: 1,300 total square feet
Foundation: Crawl space foundation, drawings also include basement and slab foundations
Price Code: A

Special features

- Combination kitchen/dining area creates an open atmosphere
- Isolated master bedroom has a private bath
- Kitchen includes a side entrance, pantry, closet and convenient laundry area
- 4 bedrooms, 2 baths

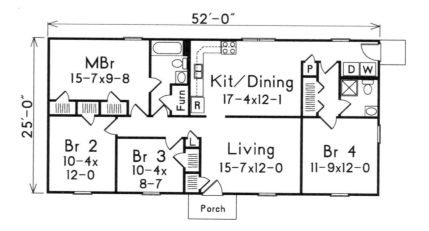

Floor plan labels:
52'-0"
25'-0"
MBr 15-7x9-8
Kit/Dining 17-4x12-1
Br 2 10-4x12-0
Br 3 10-4x8-7
Living 15-7x12-0
Br 4 11-9x12-0
Porch
Furn

Plan #528-001D-0093

Convenient Ranch

Living Area: 1,120 total square feet
Foundation: Crawl space foundation, drawings also include basement and slab foundations
Price Code: AA

Special features

- Master bedroom includes a half bath with laundry area, linen closet and kitchen access
- Kitchen has charming double-door entry, breakfast bar and a convenient walk-in pantry
- Welcoming front porch opens to large living room with coat closet
- 3 bedrooms, 1 1/2 baths

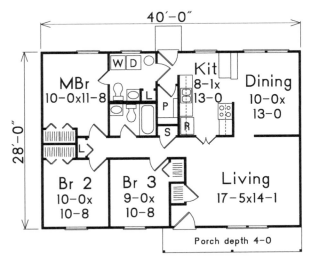

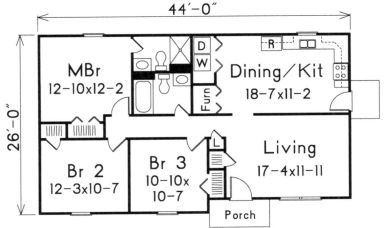

Plan #528-001D-0043

Spacious Dining And Living Areas

Living Area: 1,104 total square feet
Foundation: Crawl space foundation, drawings also include basement and slab foundations
Price Code: AA

Special features

- Master bedroom includes a private bath
- Convenient side entrance to the dining area/kitchen
- Laundry area is located near the kitchen
- Large living area creates a comfortable atmosphere
- 3 bedrooms, 2 baths

Plan #528-045D-0012

Open Layout Ensures Easy Living

Living Area: 976 total square feet
Foundation: Basement foundation
Price Code: AA

Special features

- Cozy front porch opens into large living room
- Convenient half bath is located on first floor
- All bedrooms are located on second floor for privacy
- Dining room has access to the outdoors
- 3 bedrooms, 1 1/2 baths

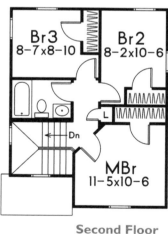

Second Floor
488 sq. ft.

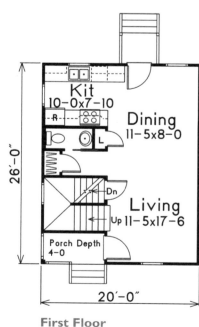

First Floor
488 sq. ft.

Plan #528-001D-0088

Ideal For A Starter Home

Living Area: 800 total square feet
Foundation: Crawl space foundation, drawings also include basement foundations
Price Code: AAA

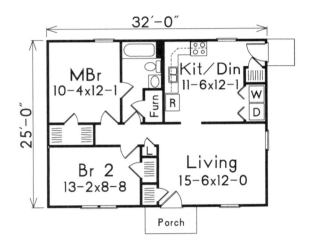

Special features

- Master bedroom has a walk-in closet and private access to the bath
- Large living room features a handy coat closet
- Kitchen includes side entrance, closet and convenient laundry area
- 2 bedrooms, 1 bath

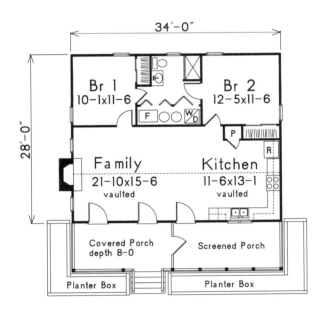

Plan #528-058D-0004

Large Vaulted Living Space

Living Area: 962 total square feet
Foundation: Crawl space foundation
Price Code: AA

Special features

- Both the kitchen and family room share warmth from the fireplace
- Charming facade features covered porch on one side, screened porch on the other and attractive planter boxes
- L-shaped kitchen boasts a convenient pantry
- 2 bedrooms, 1 bath

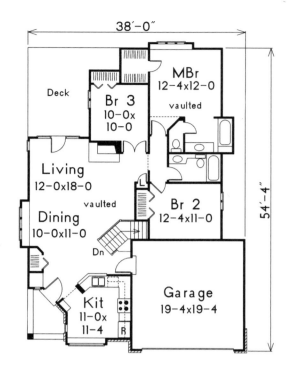

38'-0"

Deck

MBr
12-4x12-0
vaulted

Br 3
10-0x
10-0

Living
12-0x18-0

vaulted

Br 2
12-4x11-0

Dining
10-0x11-0

Dn

54'-4"

Kit
11-0x
11-4

Garage
19-4x19-4

Plan #528-022D-0022

Perfect Fit For A Narrow Site ✗

Living Area: 1,270 total square feet
Foundation: Basement foundation
Price Code: A

Special features

- Spacious living area features angled stairs, vaulted ceiling, exciting fireplace and deck access
- Master bedroom includes a walk-in closet and private bath
- Dining and living rooms join to create an open atmosphere
- Eat-in kitchen has a convenient pass-through to dining room
- 3 bedrooms, 2 baths, 2-car garage

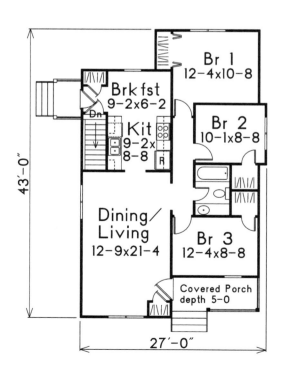

Brkfst
9-2x6-2

Dn

Br 1
12-4x10-8

Kit
9-2x
8-8

Br 2
10-1x8-8

43'-0"

Dining/
Living
12-9x21-4

Br 3
12-4x8-8

Covered Porch
depth 5-0

27'-0"

Plan #528-045D-0014

Compact Home Maximizes Space

Living Area: 987 total square feet
Foundation: Basement foundation
Price Code: AA

Special features

- Galley kitchen opens into cozy breakfast room
- Convenient coat closets are located by both entrances
- Dining/living room offers an expansive open area
- Breakfast room has access to the outdoors
- Front porch is great for enjoying outdoor living
- 3 bedrooms, 1 bath

Plan #528-040D-0026

Cozy Front Porch Welcomes Guests

Living Area: 1,393 total square feet
Foundation: Crawl space foundation, drawings also include slab foundation
Price Code: B

Special features

- L-shaped kitchen features a walk-in pantry, island cooktop and is convenient to the laundry room and dining area
- Master bedroom features a large walk-in closet and private bath with separate tub and shower
- Convenient storage/coat closet in hall
- View to the patio from the dining area
- 3 bedrooms, 2 baths, 2-car detached garage

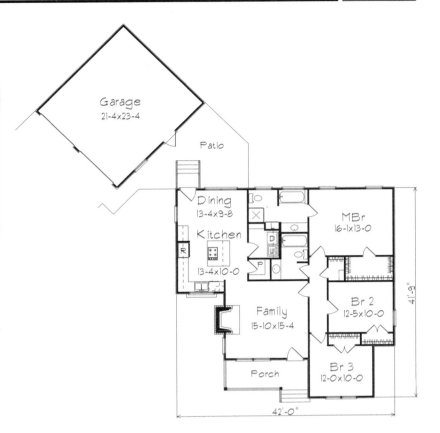

Plan #528-058D-0029

Rustic Design With Modern Features

Living Area: 1,000 total square feet
Foundation: Crawl space foundation
Price Code: AA

Special features

- Large mud room with separate covered porch entrance
- Full-length covered front porch
- Bedrooms are on opposite sides of the home for privacy
- Vaulted ceiling creates an open and spacious feeling
- 2 bedrooms, 1 bath

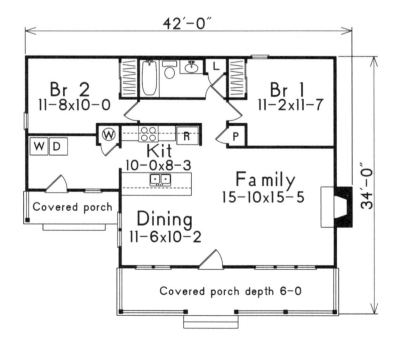

Plan #528-040D-0014

Covered Porch Is Focal Point Of Entry

Living Area: 1,595 total square feet
Foundation: Slab foundation, drawings also include crawl space foundation
Price Code: B

Special features

- Dining room has convenient built-in desk and provides access to the outdoors
- L-shaped kitchen area features island cooktop
- Family room has high ceiling and a fireplace
- Private master bedroom includes large walk-in closet and bath with separate tub and shower units
- 3 bedrooms, 2 baths, 2-car side entry garage

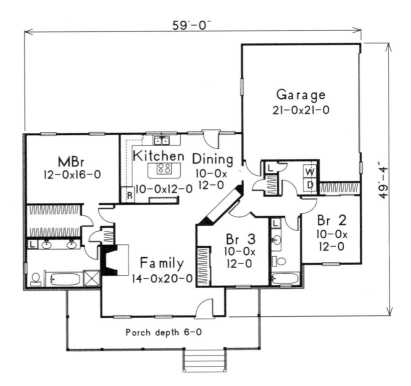

Plan #528-058D-0031

Great Design For Vacation Home Or Year-Round Living

Living Area: 990 total square feet
Foundation: Crawl space foundation
Price Code: AA

Special features

- Covered front porch adds charming feel
- Vaulted ceilings in kitchen, family and dining rooms create a spacious feel
- Large linen, pantry and storage closets throughout
- 2 bedrooms, 1 bath

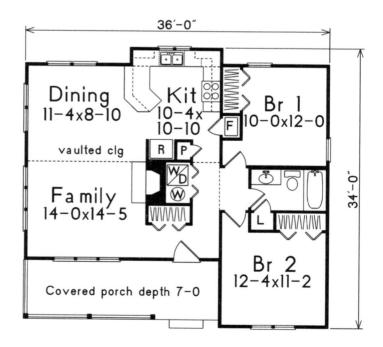

36'-0"

Dining
11-4x8-10

Kit
10-4x
10-10

Br 1
10-0x12-0

vaulted clg

R   P

F

W
D

W

Family
14-0x14-5

L

34'-0"

Br 2
12-4x11-2

Covered porch depth 7-0

Plan #528-001D-0045

Country-Style With Spacious Rooms

Living Area: 1,197 total square feet
Foundation: Crawl space foundation, drawings also include basement and slab foundations
Price Code: AA

Special features

- U-shaped kitchen includes ample workspace, breakfast bar, laundry area and direct access to the outdoors
- Large living room with convenient coat closet
- Bedroom #1 features a large walk-in closet
- 3 bedrooms, 1 bath

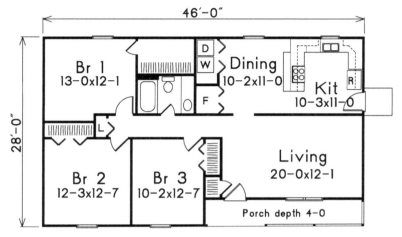

46'-0"
28'-0"

Br 1
13-0x12-1

D
W
F

Dining
10-2x11-0

Kit
10-3x11-0
R

L

Br 2
12-3x12-7

Br 3
10-2x12-7

Living
20-0x12-1

Porch depth 4-0

Plan #528-053D-0029

Compact Home For Functional Living

Living Area: 1,220 total square feet
Foundation: Basement foundation
Price Code: A

Special features

- Vaulted ceilings add luxury to the living room and master bedroom
- Spacious living room is accented with a large fireplace and hearth
- Gracious dining area is adjacent to the convenient wrap-around kitchen
- Washer and dryer are handy to the bedrooms
- Covered porch entry adds appeal
- Rear deck adjoins dining area
- 3 bedrooms, 2 baths, 2-car drive under garage

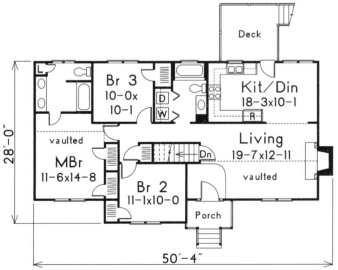

Deck

L

Br 3
10-0x 10-1

D
W

Kit/Din
18-3x10-1
R

28'-0"

vaulted

Living
19-7x12-11

MBr
11-6x14-8

Dn

vaulted

Br 2
11-1x10-0

Porch

50'-4"

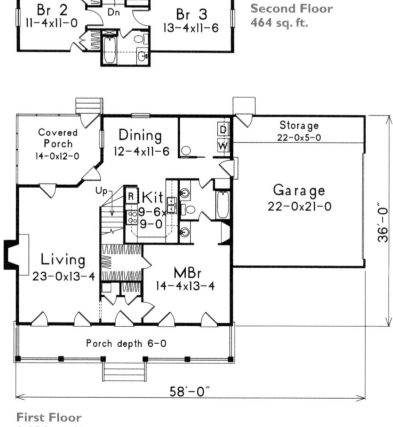

Plan #528-021D-0016

Roomy Two-Story Has Covered Porch

Living Area: 1,600 total square feet
Foundation: Crawl space foundation, drawings also include slab foundation
Price Code: B

Special features

- Energy efficient home with 2" x 6" exterior walls
- First floor master bedroom is accessible from two points of entry
- Master bath dressing area includes separate vanities and a mirrored makeup counter
- Second floor bedrooms have generous storage space and share a full bath
- 3 bedrooms, 2 baths, 2-car side entry garage

Plan #528-010D-0005

Stonework Entry Adds Character To This Home

Living Area: 1,358 total square feet
Foundation: Slab foundation
Price Code: A

Special features

- Vaulted master bath has a walk-in closet, double-bowl vanity, large tub, shower and toilet area
- Galley kitchen opens to both the living room and the breakfast area
- Vaulted ceiling joins the dining and living rooms
- Breakfast room has a full wall of windows
- 3 bedrooms, 2 baths, 2-car garage

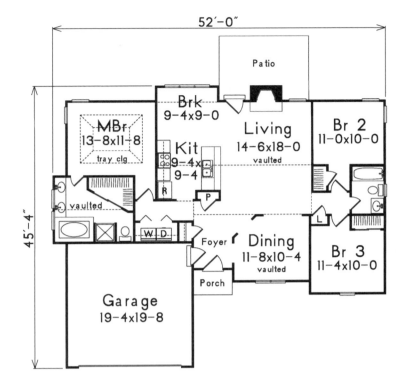

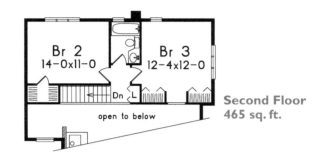

Second Floor
465 sq. ft.

Plan #528-017D-0009

Dramatic Sloping Ceiling In Living Room

Living Area: 1,432 total square feet
Foundation: Basement foundation, drawings also include slab foundation
Price Code: B

Special features

- Enter the two-story foyer from the covered porch or garage
- Living room has a square bay window with seat, glazed end wall with floor-to-ceiling windows and access to the deck
- Kitchen/dining room also opens to the deck for added convenience
- 3 bedrooms, 2 baths, 1-car garage

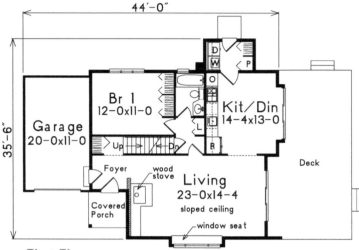

First Floor
967 sq. ft.

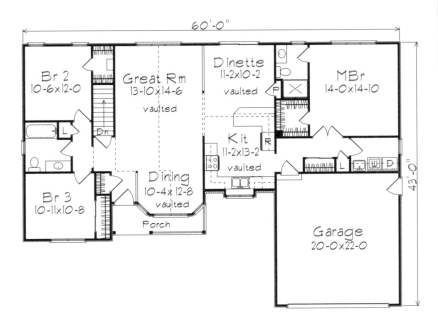

Central Living Area
Keeps Bedrooms Private

Living Area: 1,546 total square feet
Foundation: Basement foundation
Price Code: C

Special features

- Spacious, open rooms create a casual atmosphere
- Master bedroom is secluded for privacy
- Dining room features a large bay window
- Kitchen and dinette combine for added space and include access to the outdoors
- Large laundry room includes a convenient sink
- 3 bedrooms, 2 baths, 2-car garage

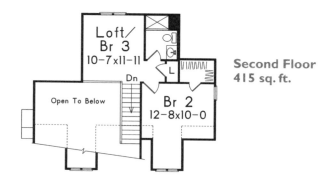

Loft/
Br 3
10-7x11-11

Open To Below

Dn

L

Br 2
12-8x10-0

Second Floor
415 sq. ft.

Plan #528-058D-0020

Surrounding Porch For Country Views

Living Area: 1,428 total square feet
Foundation: Basement foundation
Price Code: A

Special features

- Large vaulted family room opens to dining area and kitchen with breakfast bar
- First floor master bedroom offers large bath, walk-in closet and nearby laundry facilities
- A spacious loft/bedroom #3 overlooking the family room and an additional bedroom and bath complement the second floor
- 3 bedrooms, 2 baths

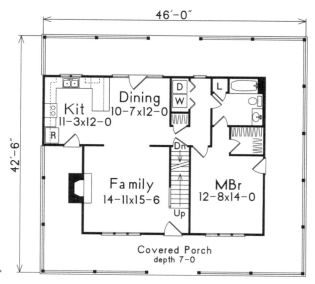

46'-0"

42'-6"

Kit
11-3x12-0

Dining
10-7x12-0

D
W

L

Family
14-11x15-6

Dn

MBr
12-8x14-0

Up

Covered Porch
depth 7-0

First Floor
1,013 sq. ft.

Plan #528-001D-0067

Layout Creates Large Open Living Area

Living Area: 1,285 total square feet
Foundation: Crawl space foundation, drawings also include basement and slab foundations
Price Code: B

Special features

- Accommodating home with ranch-style porch
- Large storage area on back of home
- Master bedroom includes dressing area, private bath and built-in bookcase
- Kitchen features pantry, breakfast bar and complete view to the dining room
- 3 bedrooms, 2 baths

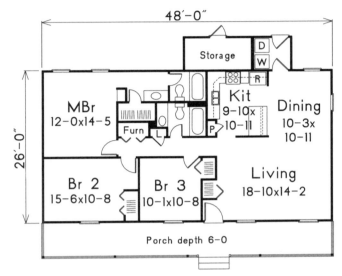

Plan #528-001D-0081

Large Great Room And Dining Area

Living Area: 1,160 total square feet
Foundation: Crawl space foundation, drawings also include basement and slab foundations
Price Code: AA

Special features

- U-shaped kitchen includes breakfast bar and convenient laundry area
- Master bedroom features private half bath and large closet
- Dining room has outdoor access
- Dining and great rooms combine to create an open living atmosphere
- 3 bedrooms, 1 1/2 baths

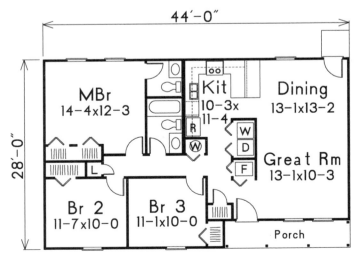

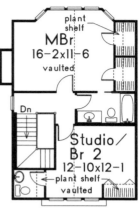

plant
shelf

MBr
16-2x11-6
vaulted

Dn

**Studio/
Br 2**
12-10x12-1
← plant shelf
vaulted

**Second Floor
576 sq. ft.**

Plan #528-007D-0032

Trendsetting Appeal
For A Narrow Lot

Living Area: 1,294 total square feet
Foundation: Basement foundation
Price Code: A

Special features

- Great room features a fireplace and large bay with windows and patio doors
- Enjoy a laundry room immersed in light with large windows, arched transom and attractive planter box
- Vaulted master bedroom features a bay window and two walk-in closets
- Bedroom #2 boasts a vaulted ceiling, plant shelf and half bath, perfect for a studio
- 2 bedrooms, 1 full bath, 2 half baths, 1-car rear entry garage

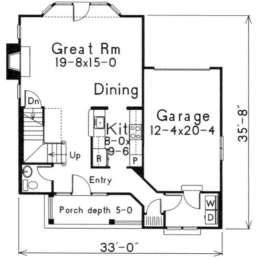

Great Rm
19-8x15-0

Dn

Dining

Kit
8-0x
9-6

Up
R   P

Entry

Porch depth 5-0
W
D

Garage
12-4x20-4

35'-8"

33'-0"

**First Floor
718 sq. ft.**

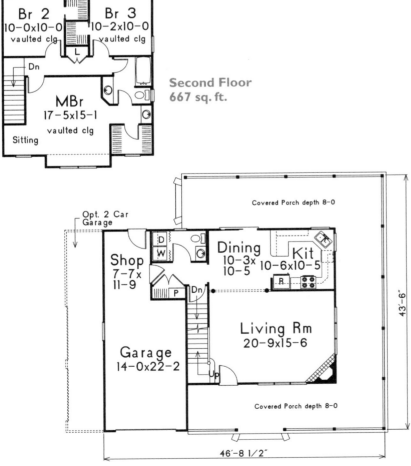

Br 2
10-0x10-0
vaulted clg

Br 3
10-2x10-0
vaulted clg

Dn

MBr
17-5x15-1
vaulted clg

Sitting

Second Floor
667 sq. ft.

Opt. 2 Car Garage

D
W

P   Dn

Shop
7-7x
11-9

Dining
10-3x
10-5

Kit
10-6x10-5

R.

Garage
14-0x22-2

Up

Living Rm
20-9x15-6

Covered Porch depth 8-0

Covered Porch depth 8-0

43'-6"

46'-8 1/2"

First Floor
732 sq. ft.

Plan #528-068D-0006

Covered Porch Surrounds Home

Living Area: 1,399 total square feet
Foundation: Basement foundation, drawings also include crawl space and slab foundations
Price Code: A

Special features

- Living room overlooks dining area through arched columns
- Laundry room contains handy half bath
- Spacious master bedroom includes sitting area, walk-in closet and plenty of sunlight
- 3 bedrooms, 1 1/2 baths, 1-car garage

Plan #528-023D-0016

Charming Home Arranged For Open Living

Living Area: 1,609 total square feet

Foundation: Slab foundation

Price Code: B

Special features

- Kitchen captures full use of space with pantry, ample cabinets and workspace
- Master bedroom is well-secluded with a walk-in closet and private bath
- Large utility room includes a sink and extra storage
- Attractive bay window in the dining area provides light
- 3 bedrooms, 2 1/2 baths, 2-car garage

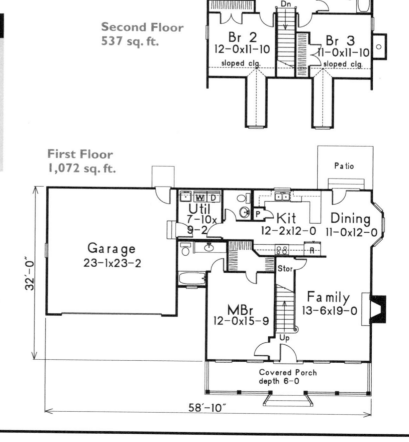

Second Floor
537 sq. ft.

attic

Br 2
12-0x11-10
sloped clg.

Br 3
11-0x11-10
sloped clg.

Dn

First Floor
1,072 sq. ft.

Patio

Util
7-10x
9-2

Kit
12-2x12-0

Dining
11-0x12-0

Garage
23-1x23-2

Stor

Family
13-6x19-0

MBr
12-0x15-9

Up

32'-0"

Covered Porch
depth 6-0

58'-10"

Plan #528-010D-0006

Brick And Siding Enhance This Traditional Home

Living Area: 1,170 total square feet
Foundation: Slab foundation
Price Code: AA

Special features

- Master bedroom enjoys privacy at the rear of this home
- Kitchen has an angled bar that overlooks great room and breakfast area
- Living areas combine to create a greater sense of spaciousness
- Great room has a cozy fireplace
- 3 bedrooms, 2 baths, 2-car garage

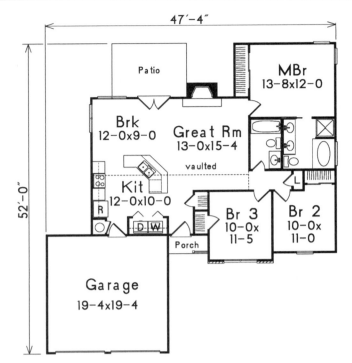

Plan #528-001D-0029

Central Fireplace Brightens Family Living

Living Area: 1,260 total square feet
Foundation: Basement foundation, drawings also include crawl space and slab foundations
Price Code: A

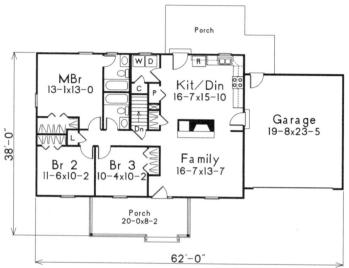

Special features

- Spacious kitchen and dining area feature a large pantry, storage area, easy access to garage and laundry room
- Pleasant covered front porch adds a practical touch
- Master bedroom with a private bath adjoins two other bedrooms, all with plenty of closet space
- 3 bedrooms, 2 baths, 2-car garage

Plan #528-053D-0035

Well Arranged For Cozy Open Living

Living Area: 1,527 total square feet
Foundation: Basement foundation, drawings also include slab and crawl space foundations
Price Code: B

Special features

- Convenient laundry room is located off the garage
- Vaulted ceiling in living room slopes to foyer and dining area creating a spacious entrance
- Galley kitchen provides easy passage to both breakfast and dining areas
- Master bedroom is complete with a large master bath, platform tub and shower, plus roomy walk-in closets
- 3 bedrooms, 2 baths, 2-car side entry garage

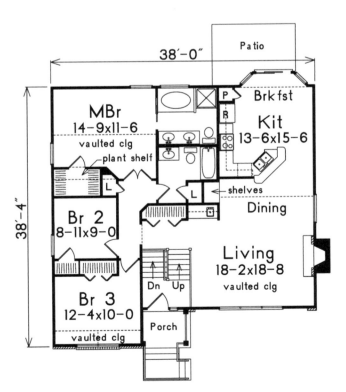

38'-0"

Patio

MBr
14-9x11-6
vaulted clg

plant shelf

Brk fst

Kit
13-6x15-6

38'-4"

Br 2
8-11x9-0

shelves

Dining

L

Br 3
12-4x10-0
vaulted clg

Dn Up

Living
18-2x18-8
vaulted clg

Porch

Plan #528-007D-0061

Distinctive Home For Sloping Terrain

Living Area: 1,340 total square feet
Foundation: Basement foundation
Price Code: A

Special features

- Grand-sized vaulted living and dining rooms offer fireplace, wet bar and breakfast counter open to spacious kitchen
- Vaulted master bedroom features a double-door entry, walk-in closet and an elegant bath
- Basement includes a huge two-car garage and space for a bedroom/bath expansion
- 3 bedrooms, 2 baths, 2-car drive under garage with storage area

Plan #528-001D-0024

Functional Layout For Comfortable Living

Living Area: 1,360 total square feet
Foundation: Basement foundation, drawings also include crawl space and slab foundations
Price Code: A

Special features

- Kitchen/dining room features island workspace and plenty of dining area
- Master bedroom has a large walk-in closet and private bath
- Laundry room is adjacent to the kitchen for easy access
- Convenient workshop in garage
- Large closets in secondary bedrooms
- 3 bedrooms, 2 baths, 2-car side entry garage

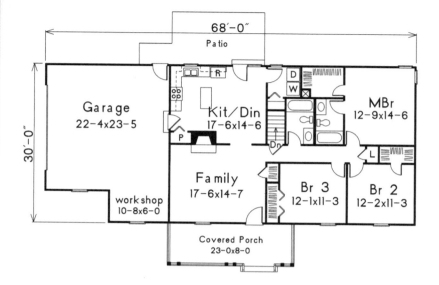

Plan #528-023D-0019

Spacious And Centrally Located Family Area

Living Area: 1,539 total square feet
Foundation: Slab foundation
Price Code: B

Special features

- Large master bedroom has a private bath with access to patio
- Convenient laundry room is located between carport and kitchen
- Bedrooms are secluded from living areas for added privacy
- Private dining area features a bay window for elegant entertaining
- Attached carport offers an additional roomy storage area
- 3 bedrooms, 2 baths, 2-car attached carport

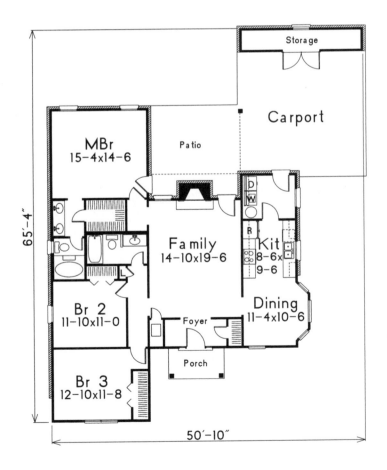

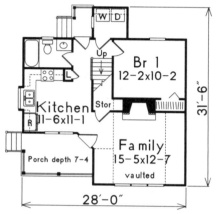

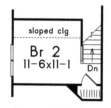

Second Floor
168 sq. ft.

First Floor
660 sq. ft.

28'-0"

31'-6"

W D

Up

Br 1
12-2x10-2

Kitchen
11-6x11-1

Stor

Family
15-5x12-7
vaulted

Porch depth 7-4

sloped clg

Br 2
11-6x11-1

Dn

Plan #528-040D-0028

Cottage-Style, Appealing And Cozy

Living Area: 828 total square feet
Foundation: Crawl space foundation
Price Code: AAA

Special features

- Vaulted ceiling in living area enhances space
- Convenient laundry room
- Sloped ceiling creates unique style in bedroom #2
- Efficient storage space under the stairs
- Covered entry porch provides cozy sitting area and plenty of shade
- 2 bedrooms, 1 bath

Plan #528-058D-0033

Flexible Design Is Popular

Living Area: 1,440 total square feet
Foundation: Basement foundation
Price Code: A

Special features

- Open floor plan with access to covered porches in front and back
- Lots of linen, pantry and closet space throughout
- Laundry/mud room between kitchen and garage is a convenient feature
- 2 bedrooms, 2 baths, 2-car side entry garage

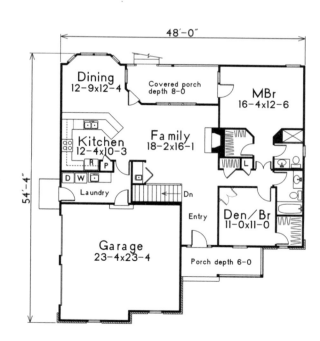

48'-0"

54'-4"

Dining
12-9x12-4

Covered porch
depth 8-0

MBr
16-4x12-6

Kitchen
12-4x10-3

Family
18-2x16-1

L

Laundry

DW

R P

Dn

Entry

Den/Br
11-0x11-0

Garage
23-4x23-4

Porch depth 6-0

Home Plans Index

Plan Number	Square Feet	Price Code	Page	Plan Number	Square Feet	Price Code	Page	Plan Number	Square Feet	Price Code	Page
528-001D-0018	988	AA	43	528-007D-0042	914	AA	7	528-040D-0014	1,595	B	59
528-001D-0021	1,416	A	26	528-007D-0049	1,791	C	9	528-040D-0026	1,393	B	57
528-001D-0023	1,343	A	26	528-007D-0054	1,575	B	5	528-040D-0027	1,597	C	28
528-001D-0024	1,360	A	74	528-007D-0060	1,268	B	15	528-040D-0028	828	AAA	76
528-001D-0029	1,260	A	72	528-007D-0061	1,340	A	73	528-040D-0029	1,028	AA	17
528-001D-0030	1,416	A	31	528-007D-0067	1,761	B	6	528-041D-0004	1,195	AA	43
528-001D-0031	1,501	B	3	528-007D-0068	1,384	B	18	528-045D-0012	976	AA	54
528-001D-0040	864	AAA	21	528-007D-0070	929	AA	14	528-045D-0014	987	AA	56
528-001D-0041	1,000	AA	41	528-007D-0073	902	AA	50	528-045D-0017	954	AA	36
528-001D-0043	1,104	AA	53	528-007D-0075	1,684	B	33	528-053D-0002	1,668	C	20
528-001D-0045	1,197	AA	61	528-007D-0102	1,452	A	16	528-053D-0029	1,220	A	61
528-001D-0067	1,285	B	67	528-007D-0105	1,084	AA	30	528-053D-0035	1,527	B	72
528-001D-0069	1,504	B	39	528-007D-0107	1,161	AA	30	528-053D-0044	1,340	A	29
528-001D-0072	1,288	A	35	528-010D-0005	1,358	A	63	528-058D-0003	1,020	AA	31
528-001D-0077	1,769	B	10	528-010D-0006	1,170	AA	71	528-058D-0004	962	AA	55
528-001D-0081	1,160	AA	67	528-010D-0007	1,427	A	49	528-058D-0006	1,339	A	24
528-001D-0086	1,154	AA	48	528-017D-0007	1,567	C	19	528-058D-0010	676	AAA	37
528-001D-0087	1,230	A	44	528-017D-0008	1,466	B	32	528-058D-0012	1,143	AA	40
528-001D-0088	800	AAA	55	528-017D-0009	1,432	B	64	528-058D-0013	1,073	AA	34
528-001D-0090	1,300	A	52	528-017D-0010	1,660	C	38	528-058D-0016	1,558	B	47
528-001D-0091	1,334	A	40	528-021D-0016	1,600	B	62	528-058D-0020	1,428	A	66
528-001D-0092	1,664	B	27	528-022D-0001	1,039	AA	22	528-058D-0021	1,477	A	42
528-001D-0093	1,120	AA	53	528-022D-0018	1,368	A	52	528-058D-0022	1,578	B	42
528-005D-0001	1,400	B	8	528-022D-0019	1,283	A	51	528-058D-0024	1,598	B	29
528-007D-0028	1,711	B	13	528-022D-0022	1,270	A	56	528-058D-0029	1,000	AA	58
528-007D-0031	1,092	AA	25	528-022D-0024	1,127	AA	35	528-058D-0030	990	AA	21
528-007D-0032	1,294	A	68	528-023D-0016	1,609	B	70	528-058D-0031	990	AA	60
528-007D-0036	1,330	A	23	528-023D-0019	1,539	B	75	528-058D-0033	1,440	A	76
528-007D-0037	1,403	A	11	528-033D-0012	1,546	C	65	528-068D-0003	1,784	B	45
528-007D-0038	1,524	B	46	528-037D-0017	829	AAA	39	528-068D-0006	1,399	A	69
528-007D-0041	1,700	B	4	528-040D-0003	1,475	B	12				

What Kind Of Plan Package Do You Need?

Now that you've found the home you've been looking for, here are some suggestions on how to make your Dream Home a reality. To get started, order the type of plans that fit your particular situation.

YOUR CHOICES:

The 1-Set Study package - We offer a 1-set plan package so you can study your home in detail. This one set is considered a study set and is marked "not for construction." It is a copyright violation to reproduce blueprints.

The Minimum 5-Set package - If you're ready to start the construction process, this 5-set package is the minimum number of blueprint sets you will need. It will require keeping close track of each set so they can be used by multiple subcontractors and tradespeople.

The Standard 8-set package - For best results in terms of cost, schedule and quality of construction, we recommend you order eight (or more) sets of blueprints. Besides one set for yourself, additional sets of blueprints will be required by your mortgage lender, local building department, general contractor and all subcontractors working on foundation, electrical, plumbing, heating/air conditioning, carpentry work, etc.

Reproducible Masters - If you wish to make some minor design changes, you'll want to order reproducible masters. These drawings contain the same information as the blueprints but are printed on erasable and reproducible paper. This will allow your builder or a local design professional to make the necessary drawing changes without the major expense of redrawing the plans. This package also allows you to print as many copies of the modified plans as you need.

Mirror Reverse Sets - Plans can be printed in mirror reverse. These plans are useful when the house would fit your site better if all the rooms were on the opposite side than shown. They are simply a mirror image of the original drawings causing the lettering and dimensions to read backwards. Therefore, when ordering mirror reverse drawings, you must purchase at least one set of right-reading plans.

Our Blueprint Packages Offer...

Quality plans for building your future, with extras that provide unsurpassed value, ensure good construction and long-term enjoyment.

A quality home - one that looks good, functions well, and provides years of enjoyment - is a product of many things - design, materials, craftsmanship. But it's also the result of outstanding blueprints - the actual plans and specifications that tell the builder exactly how to build your home.

And with our BLUEPRINT PACKAGES you get the absolute best. A complete set of blueprints is available for every design in this book. These "working drawings," are highly detailed, resulting in two key benefits:

- Better understanding by the contractor of how to build your home, and...

- More accurate construction estimates.

When you purchase one of our designs, you'll receive all of the BLUEPRINT components shown here - elevations, foundation plan, floor plans, sections and/or details. Other helpful building aids are also available to help make your dream home a reality.

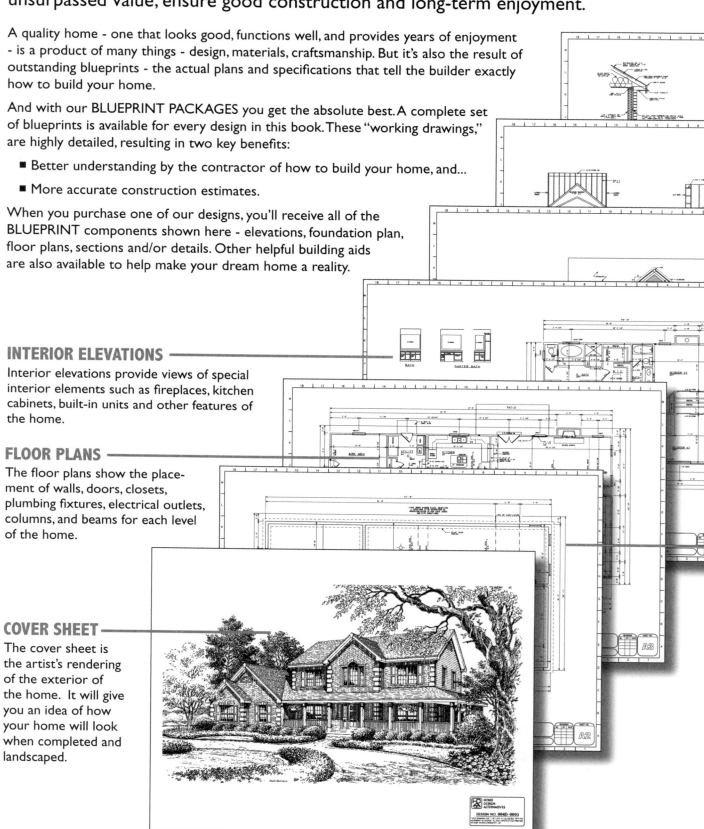

INTERIOR ELEVATIONS

Interior elevations provide views of special interior elements such as fireplaces, kitchen cabinets, built-in units and other features of the home.

FLOOR PLANS

The floor plans show the placement of walls, doors, closets, plumbing fixtures, electrical outlets, columns, and beams for each level of the home.

COVER SHEET

The cover sheet is the artist's rendering of the exterior of the home. It will give you an idea of how your home will look when completed and landscaped.

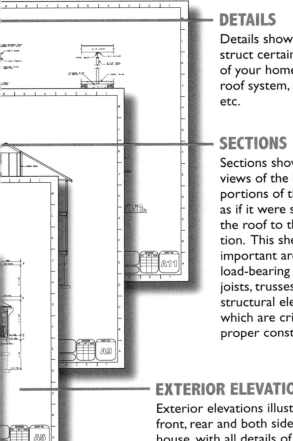

DETAILS

Details show how to construct certain components of your home, such as the roof system, stairs, deck, etc.

SECTIONS

Sections show detail views of the home or portions of the home as if it were sliced from the roof to the foundation. This sheet shows important areas such as load-bearing walls, stairs, joists, trusses and other structural elements, which are critical for proper construction.

EXTERIOR ELEVATIONS

Exterior elevations illustrate the front, rear and both sides of the house, with all details of exterior materials and the required dimensions.

FOUNDATION PLAN

The foundation plan shows the layout of the basement, crawl space, slab or pier foundation. All necessary notations and dimensions are included. See plan page for the foundation types included. If the home plan you choose does not have your desired foundation type, our Customer Service Representatives can advise you on how to customize your foundation to suit your specific needs or site conditions.

GENERAL BUILDING SPECIFICATIONS

This document outlines the technical requirements for proper construction such as the strength of materials, insulation ratings, allowable loading conditions, etc.

Other Helpful Building Aids...

Your Blueprint Package will contain the necessary construction information to build your home. We also offer the following products and services to save you time and money in the building process.

MATERIAL LIST

Material lists are available for all the plans in this book. Each list gives you the quantity, dimensions and description of the building materials necessary to construct your home. You'll get faster and more accurate bids from your contractor while saving money by paying for only the materials you need. Cost: $125

DETAIL PLAN PACKAGES:

Framing, Plumbing & Electrical Plan Packages
Three separate packages offer homebuilders details for constructing various foundations; numerous floor, wall and roof framing techniques; simple to complex residential wiring; sump and water softener hookups; plumbing connection methods; installation of septic systems and more. Each package includes three-dimensional illustrations and a glossary of terms. Purchase one or all three. Cost: $20.00 each or all three for $40.00. Note: These drawings do not pertain to a specific home plan.

THE LEGAL KIT ™

Our Legal Kit provides contracts and legal forms to help protect you from the potential pitfalls inherent in the building process. The Kit supplies commonly used forms and contracts suitable for homeowners and builders. It can save you a considerable amount of time and help protect you and your assets during and after construction. Cost: $35.00.

EXPRESS DELIVERY

Most orders are processed within 24 hours of receipt. Please allow 7-10 business days for delivery. If you need to place a rush order, please call us by 11:00 a.m. Monday-Friday CST and ask for express service (allow 1-2 business days).

TECHNICAL ASSISTANCE

If you have questions, call our technical support line at 1-314-770-2228 between 8:00 a.m. and 5:00 p.m. Monday-Friday CST. Whether it involves design modifications or field assistance, our designers are extremely familiar with all of our designs and will be happy to help you. We want your home to be everything you expect it to be.

 HOME DESIGN ALTERNATIVES, INC.

How To Order

For fastest service, Call Toll-Free
1-800-DREAM HOME
(1-800-373-2646) day or night

Three Easy Ways To Order

1. CALL toll-free 1-800-373-2646 for credit card orders. MasterCard, Visa, Discover and American Express are accepted.

2. FAX your order to 1-314-770-2226.

3. MAIL the Order Form to:

   HDA, Inc.
   944 Anglum Road
   St. Louis, MO 63042

Order Form

Please send me -
PLAN NUMBER   528 - _____

PRICE CODE _____ *(see page 77)*

Specify Foundation Type *(see plan page for availability)*
- ☐ Slab ☐ Crawl space ☐ Pier
- ☐ Basement ☐ Walk-out basement

☐ Reproducible Masters	$ _____
☐ Eight-Set Plan Package	$ _____
☐ Five-Set Plan Package	$ _____
☐ One-Set Study Package *(no mirror reverse)*	$ _____
☐ Additional Plan Sets*	
_____ (Qty.) at $45.00 each	$ _____
☐ Print in Mirror Reverse	
_____ (Qty.) at $15.00 each	$ _____
☐ Material List* $125 *(see page 79)*	$ _____
☐ Legal Kit *(see page 79)*	$ _____

Detail Plan Packages: *(see page 79)*

☐ Framing ☐ Electrical ☐ Plumbing	$ _____
SUBTOTAL	$ _____
Sales Tax - MO residents add 6%	$ _____
☐ Shipping / Handling *(see chart at right)*	$ _____
TOTAL ENCLOSED *(US funds only)*	$ _____

(Sorry no CODs)

I hereby authorize HDA, Inc. to charge this purchase to my credit card account (check one):

☐ MasterCard ☐ VISA ☐ DISCOVER NOVUS ☐ AMERICAN EXPRESS Cards

Credit Card number _____

Expiration date_____

Signature _____

Name_____
(Please print or type)

Street Address_____
*(Please **do not** use PO Box)*

City _____

State _____ Zip _____

Daytime phone number (_____) - _____

I'm a ☐ Builder/Contractor   I ☐ have
        ☐ Homeowner   ☐ have not
        ☐ Renter   selected my
                                     general contractor

Thank you for your order!
80

Important Information To Know Before You Order

- **Exchange Policies** - Since blueprints are printed in response to your order, we cannot honor requests for refunds. However, if for some reason you find that the plan you have purchased does not meet your requirements, you may exchange that plan for another plan in our collection within 90 days of purchase. At the time of the exchange, you will be charged a processing fee of 25% of your original plan package price, plus the difference in price between the plan packages (if applicable) and the cost to ship the new plans to you.

  Please note: *Reproducible drawings can only be exchanged if the package is unopened.*

- **Building Codes & Requirements** - At the time the construction drawings were prepared, every effort was made to ensure that these plans and specifications meet nationally recognized codes. Our plans conform to most national building codes. Because building codes vary from area to area, some drawing modifications and/or the assistance of a professional designer or architect may be necessary to comply with your local codes or to accommodate specific building site conditions. We advise you to consult with your local building official for information regarding codes governing your area.

Questions? Call Our Customer Service Number
314-770-2228

Blueprint Price Schedule

Price Code	1-Set	SAVE $110 5-Sets	SAVE $200 8-Sets	Reproducible Masters
AAA	$225	$295	$340	$440
AA	$325	$395	$440	$540
A	$385	$455	$500	$600
B	$445	$515	$560	$660
C	$500	$570	$615	$715
D	$560	$630	$675	$775
E	$620	$690	$735	$835
F	$675	$745	$790	$890
G	$765	$835	$880	$980
H	$890	$960	$1005	$1105

BEST VALUE

Plan prices guaranteed through June 30, 2006.
Please note that plans are not refundable.

- **Additional Sets*** - Additional sets of the plan ordered are available for $45.00 each. Five-set, eight-set, and reproducible packages offer considerable savings.

- **Mirror Reverse Plans*** - Available for an additional $15.00 per set, these plans are simply a mirror image of the original drawings causing the dimensions and lettering to read backwards. Therefore, when ordering mirror reverse plans, you must purchase at least one set of right-reading plans.

- **One-Set Study Package** - We offer a one-set plan package so you can study your home in detail. This one set is considered a study set and is marked "not for construction." It is a copyright violation to reproduce blueprints.

***Available only within 90 days after purchase of plan package or reproducible masters of same plan.**

Shipping & Handling Charges

U.S. SHIPPING - *(AK and HI - express only)*	1-4 Sets	5-7 Sets	8 Sets or Reproducibles
Regular *(allow 7-10 business days)*	$15.00	$17.50	$25.00
Priority *(allow 3-5 business days)*	$25.00	$30.00	$35.00
Express* *(allow 1-2 business days)*	$35.00	$40.00	$45.00

CANADA SHIPPING	1-4 Sets	5-7 Sets	8 Sets or Reproducibles
Standard *(allow 8-12 business days)*	$25.00	$30.00	$35.00
Express* *(allow 3-5 business days)*	$40.00	$40.00	$45.00

Overseas Shipping/International - Call, fax, or e-mail (plans@hdainc.com) for shipping costs.

* For express delivery please call us by 11:00 a.m. Monday-Friday CST